SHOPPING

London is a marvellous shopping centre. There are so many wonderful shops that it's difficult to get to them all. For this reason you'll find the shop by shop street maps, hints on what to buy, details of tax concessions and the clothes and measure conversion charts, extremely useful.

GETTING OUT 83

It's a great city and one of the best ways to get out exploring is on one of the tours. But there are also many beautiful and exciting places outside London – historic towns and lordly country houses, all within easy reach. In this section you'll also find all the means of transport out of London, including rail terminals, and airports for those who are travelling even further afield.

INFORMATION 92

Everything you need to know to keep you going – banks and foreign exchange, tourist offices, passports, telephone services, tips on tips and where to find hotel accommodation – even how to get hold of emergency services. Relax. You've got London in your pocket.

Symbols

L	lunch	
D	dinner	
B	buffet	

Average prices for a meal without wine:

£	Under £5.00 per person
££	Under £10.00 per person
£££	Under £15 per person
£££+	Over £15 per person
Children	Children welcome, sometimes with a reduction in price.
Reserve	It is advisable to reserve
M	Membership necessary
A	Access
Ax	American Express
B	Barclaycard

Cb	Carte Blanche
Dc	Diners Club
E	Eurocard
	Mastercharge – Interbank can be used where you see the Access sign, and Visa at the Barclaycard sign.

Opening times

Many places are closed on Xmas, New Year and Good Friday, and general opening times are subject to change so it may be advisable to check first.

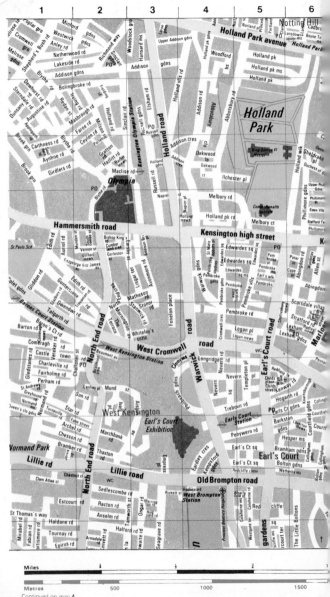

Continued on map 4

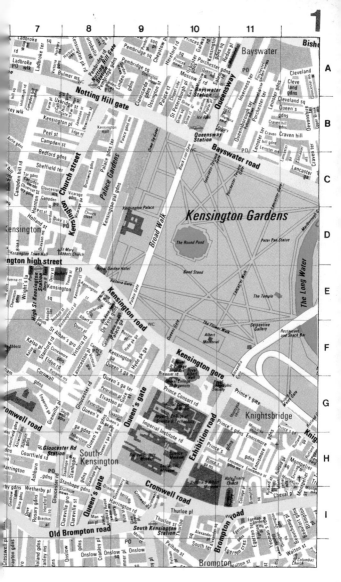

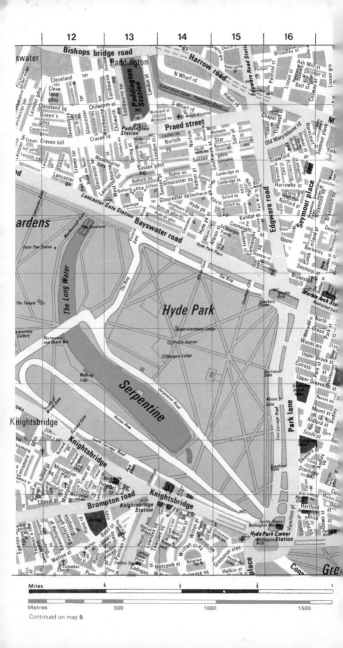

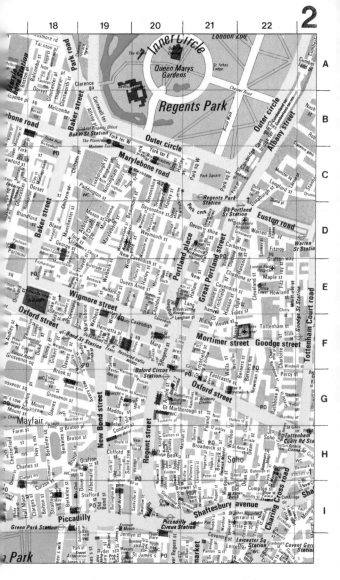

Miles

Metres   500   1000   1500

Continued on map 6

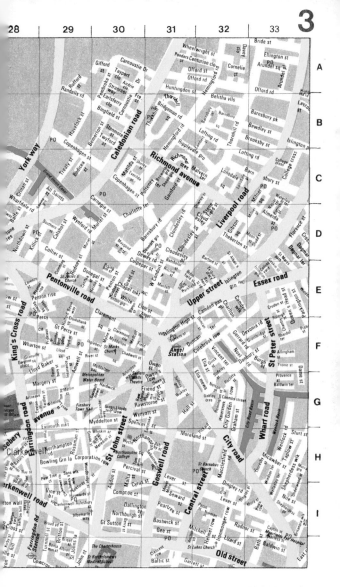

1 2 3 4 5 6

Estcourt rd
Racton rd
Tamworth
Ongar
Hild
yard rd
Station

St Thomas's way
Anselm rd

Mirabel rd
Haldane rd
Halford rd
Melrose
ton rd
Coleherne
Red
cliffe

Fabian rd
Tournay rd
Seagrave rd
Princess Beatrice Hosp
Westgate ter
sq
The Little Boltons

Hartismere rd
Epirus rd
Armadale rd
Knivett rd
Micklethwaite rd
Ifield rd
Finborough rd
Redcliffe ms
Harcourt ter
Treginter rd

Shorrolds rd
Eustace rd
Farm la
Cath
cart rd
Redcliffe
Cathcart rd

Dawes road
Walham gro
Redcliffe sq
cott st
Hollywood
Seymour wlk
Redcliffe

Bishops rd
Farm la
Walham Green
Redcliffe st
Faw
PO

Burnthwaite rd
PO
Stamford Bridge
Chelsea
Football Ground
Chapel
Netherton
Hernshaw rd
Gertrude st
Lamont r

Darlan rd
Barclay rd
Effie rd
Fulham Broadway Station
Fulham road
St Marks Coll
Gunter gro
Hortensia rd
Edith gro
Langton
Slaidburn
Lamont r

Elmstone
Shottendane rd
Harbledown rd
Cedarne rd
Fulham Town Hall
Moore pk rd
Water
Holmead
Wandon rd
Edith
ter

Novello st
Musgrave cres
Britannia
Maxwell
Gumbold rd
Kings road
Stanley

Campana rd
Kemp
son la
Eel Brook
Common
Harwood road
Avalon rd
Edith
Michael rd
Edith gro
Work End
PO
Blantyre

Basuto rd
Crondace rd
Fawcett rd
Harwood ter
Embden
Sands
Lots rd
Talcott rd
Burnaby st
Cremorne rd

Quarrendon rd
Stevenchurch
Rycroft st
Chipstead st
Bovingdon rd
Folham Gas Works
Upcerne rd
Uverdale rd
Tadema rd
Stadium st
Lots rd

Perrymead st
Bowerdean
Cresford rd
Sandilands rd
Michael rd

Clancarty rd
Studdridge st
Pearscroft rd
Bagley's la
Ful
nead
Imperial rd

Beltran rd
Langford
Dock

Ashcombe st
Canbury
Broughton rd
Gilstead rd
Furness
Maxmenring
Elswick
Ful
nead

Varborough
st
Friston
st
Oakbury
Haldvorth
Stephendale rd
Glenrosa
Ellie st
Battersea

Woolneigh st
Rosebury rd
Guerin st
Bramlands
Westbridge
rd
Bolingbroke wlk

De Morgan rd
Hamble st
Kilmaine rd
Townmead rd
Fulham Power Station
St Marks Church
Sunbury la

Althea st
Edenvale st
York Pl
Heliport
Vicarage rd
Grenfell
Parkham
st
Surrey

River Thames
Vicarage cres

Lombard rd
Harrowby
rd
Gwynne
Vicarage cres
Battersea High st
Trott st
Orbel st
Octavia st

Holman
rd
Yelverton
rd
Orville
rd
Henning
Ursula st

Simpson st
Shuttleworth rd

Winders rd
Bullen st
Patrick
pass
Home
Inworth st
Ballerin st
Stanmer st

York road
Mendip
Chatfield rd
Plough rd
Wye st
Median st
Inglewood
Newcomen
Lavender rd
Coppock
Hicks cl
Falcon rd
Patience
Afghan rd
Candahar rd
Abercrombie
Row ena cres
Cabul rd
Fretz

Hope st
Holgate st
Lavender
Winn
Stanley rd
Orbel
Magan
Sullivan
Mcdermott cl
Falcon rd
Kerrison
Warfield rd
Falcon

watergate
Wynter st
Wallis st
Fowler cl
Hicks
Dss

Miles   ¼   ½   ¾   1

Metres   500   1000   1500

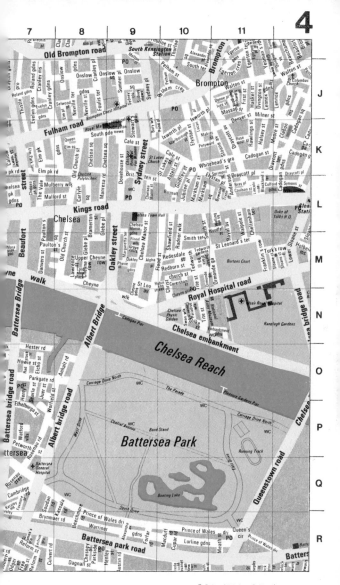

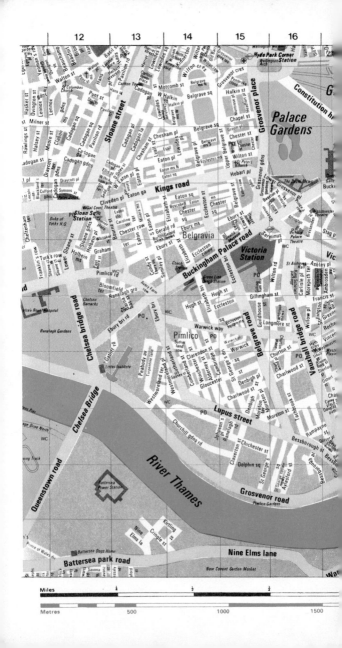

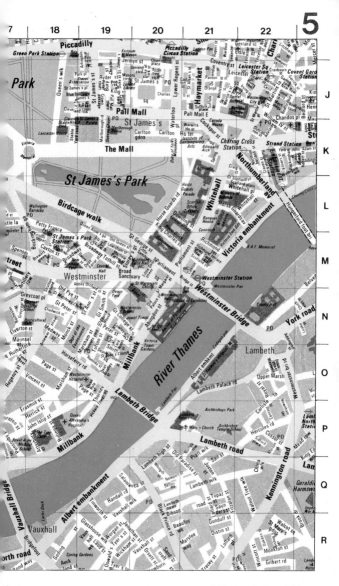

Miles

Metres   500   1000   1500

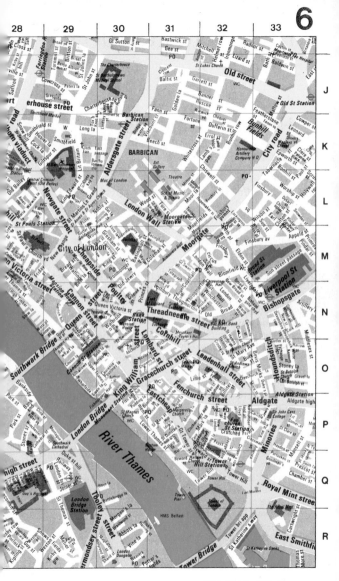

HISTORIC LONDON

Historic buildings

This list covers the most important of the historic houses, notable buildings, monuments and items of general historic interest. Look also under sections such as 'Churches' or 'Parks'.

Bank of England   **6 N 31**
Threadneedle St EC2. 01-601 4444. The vaults hold the nation's gold reserves. Outer walls are still the original design by Sir John Soane, architect to the Bank from 1788-1833. Rebuilt by Sir H. Baker 1925-39.

Buckingham Palace   **5 K 17**
St James's Pk SW1. The permanent London palace of the reigning Sovereign. Originally built 1705; remodelled by Nash 1825; refaced 1913 by Sir Aston Webb.

Burlington Arcade   **2 I 19**
Piccadilly W1. 1819 Regency shopping promenade with original shop windows. Still employs a beadle to preserve the gracious atmosphere.

Burlington House   **2 I 19**
Piccadilly W1. Victorian-Renaissance façade on one of the great 18th C palaces. Houses the Royal Academy and various Royal Societies.

Charing Cross WC2   **5 K 22**
The Charing Cross was the last of the stone crosses set up by Edward I to mark the funeral resting places of Queen Eleanor's body on its way to Westminster Abbey. Originally placed where Trafalgar Sq now is, it was demolished in 1647 and the statue of Charles I now stands in its place. The stone cross in the station courtyard is a replica.

Chelsea Royal Hospital   **4 N 11**
Chelsea Embankment SW3. A hospital for old soldiers. Fine, austere building. 1682 by Wren. Stables 1814 by Sir John Soane. Museum *OPEN 10.00-12.00 & 14.15-16.00 Mon-Fri, 14.00-16.00 Sun. Free.*

Chiswick House
Burlington La W4. 01-994 3299. Lovely Palladian villa built in the grand manner by 3rd Earl of Burlington 1725-30. Fine interiors and gardens by William

Kent. *OPEN 09.30-13.00, 14.00-16.00 15 Oct-15 Mar; to 18.30 summer months. CLOSED Mon, Tue Oct-Mar. Small charge.*

Clarence House 5 K 18
Stable Yard Gate SW1. Mansion by Nash 1825. Now the home of the Queen Mother.

College of Arms 6 M 28
Queen Victoria St EC4. 01-248 2762. Handsome late 17th C building which houses the official records of English, Welsh and Irish heraldry and genealogy. *OPEN 10.00-16.00 Mon-Fri. Appt only for parties.*

Covent Garden Market WC2 6 J 23
Originally designed by Inigo Jones (with his St Paul's church) as a residential square in the 1630s. Market buildings are of 1830 by Fowler, Floral Hall added in 1860 by E. M. Barry, architect of the Royal Opera House (1858). In 1974 the market moved to Nine Elms, but the area survived threats of redevelopment to become a flourishing new community, with a shopping centre and Transport Museum. The Theatre Museum opens 1985.

Fenton House
Hampstead Gro NW3. 01-435 3471. The Benton Fletcher collection of early keyboard instruments and the Binning collection of porcelain and furniture. *OPEN Apr-Oct 14.00-18.00 Mon-Wed, Sat & Sun. CLOSED Dec-Feb. OPEN Mar Sat & Sun only.*

Gray's Inn 3 I 27
Holborn WC1. 01-405 8164. Entrance from passage next to Holborn Bars, 22 High Holborn. An Inn of Court since 14th C. The Hall (16th C) and 'Buildings' restored after bomb damage. Gardens were laid out by Francis Bacon. *Hall OPEN by written application to the Under Treasurer. Gardens OPEN May, Jul & Oct 12.00-14.00; Aug-Sept 08.15-17.30. CLOSED Sat, Sun & B. hols. Free.*

Greenwich
Six miles down river and associated with England's former sea power. The following are notable:

Greenwich: Charlton House
Charlton Rd SE7. 01-856 3951. Perfect small red brick Jacobean manor house on an 'H' plan, built 1607-12. Fine ceilings, staircase and some bizarre chimney-pieces. Now a community centre. *Guided tours by appt only. Contact warden.*

Greenwich: The Queen's House
Romney Rd SE10. 01-858 4422. Now part of the National Maritime Museum. Built by Inigo Jones 1619 for the Queen of Denmark. *OPEN summer 10.00-18.00 Tue-Sat, 14.00-17.30 Sun; winter*

10.00-17.00 Mon-Sat, 14.00-17.00 Sun. Free.

Greenwich: Royal Hospital
Greenwich SE10. 01-858 2154. Now the Royal Naval College, the site of the former Royal palace for the Tudor Sovereigns. A fine and interesting group of classical buildings by Webb 1664, Wren 1694 and Vanbrugh 1728. Chapel by James 'Athenian' Stuart 1789 and Painted Hall by Thornhill. *OPEN 14.30-17.00. CLOSED Thur. Free.*

Greenwich: Rotunda Museum
Woolwich Common SE18. 01-856 5533 ext 385. Pavilion by Nash 1814. Little known museum full of guns of the Royal Artillery. *OPEN Apr-Oct 12.00-17.00 Mon-Fri, 13.00-17.00 Sat & Sun; Nov-Mar 12.00-16.00 Mon-Fri, 13.00-16.00 Sat & Sun. Free.*

Greenwich: Old Royal Observatory
Greenwich Pk SE10. 01-858 1167. Formerly the Greenwich Observatory. Part of the National Maritime Museum and includes Flamsteed House. Designed by Wren and founded by Charles II in 1675. Time and astronomical instruments. *OPEN summer 10.00-18.00 Tue-Sat, 14.00-17.30 Sun. Winter 10.00-17.00 Tue-Sat, 14.00-17.00 Sun.* Also a Planetarium: *OPEN summer months only*, phone for details. Consists of talks illustrated by slides.

Guildhall   **6 M 30**
Off Gresham St EC2. 01-606 3030. 15th C with façade by George Dance 1789 and later restorations by Sir Giles Gilbert Scott. The Great Hall is used for ceremonial occasions. Medieval groined vaulting in crypts. Great Hall *OPEN 10.00-17.00 Mon-Fri, 10.00-16.00 Sat & Sun. CLOSED on Sun Nov-Apr.* Library *OPEN 09.30-17.00 Mon-Sat.* Art Gallery *opening hours vary according to exhibition.*

Henry VIII's Wine Cellar   **5 L 21**
Whitehall SW1. Genuine Tudor wine cellar built for Cardinal Wolsey. All that remains of Tudor Whitehall Palace. *OPEN Sat afternoons from Mar-Sept by pass from the Dept of the Environment, Room 10/16, St Christopher House, Southwark St SE1.*

Houses of Parliament   **5 N 20**
St Margaret St SW1. 01-219 3000. Victorian-Gothic building 1840-68 by Sir Charles Barry and A. W. N. Pugin. Westminster Hall was built in 1099 as the

Great Hall of William Rufus' new palace; the roof dates from the late 14th C. *Admission to the House of Commons during debates by application to your MP or by queuing. Old Westminster Hall OPEN during session 10.00-13.30 Mon-Thur (providing neither house is sitting), 10.00-17.00 Sat. During recess 10.00-16.00 Mon-Fri, 10.00-17.00 Sat. Tours Sat and certain days during recess.*

Kensington Palace   1 D 9
Kensington Gdns W8. 01-937 9561. Unostentatious house bought in 1689 by William III and altered by Wren and William Kent; attribution of the Orangery, of exceptionally fine brick, is uncertain. Queen Victoria and Queen Mary were born here. State apartments *OPEN 09.00-17.00 Mon-Sat, 13.00-17.00 Sun. CLOSED some B. hols, Xmas Eve and Xmas. Charge.*

Lambeth Palace
Lambeth Palace Rd SE1. 01-928 6222. (Library only). The London residence of the Archbishop of Canterbury. 15th C. Fine medieval crypt and 17th C hall. Portraits from 16th-19th C. Library for readers only. *OPEN 10.00-17.00 Mon-Fri. CLOSED at conference times, Easter, B. hols and Xmas.*

Law Courts   6 K 25
Strand WC2. 01-405 7641. Massive Victorian-Gothic building, housing the Royal Courts of Justice. *OPEN to public 10.00-16.30 Mon-Fri.* Courts not in session *Aug and Sept* but open to public.

Leadenhall Market   6 O 31
Gracechurch St EC3. Impressive Victorian glass and iron hall 1881 by Horace Jones preserving the old street pattern; on the site of the Roman basilica.

Lincoln's Inn   3 I 25
Lincoln's Inn WC2. 01-405 1393. An Inn of Court. 17th C. New square, gardens, barristers' chambers and solicitors' offices. A chapel by Inigo Jones (1623) and the 15th C Old Hall. Great Hall was built in 1845. The 'Stone Buildings' are by Sir Robert Taylor and were begun in 1774. Still has Dickensian atmosphere. Gardens and Chapel *OPEN 12.00-14.30 Mon-Fri. Guided tours of Chapel by*

appt. Admission to Hall by application to the Treasury Office. Free.

Lincoln's Inn Fields WC2   **3 I 25**

7 acres of gardens laid out by Inigo Jones 1618. Once a famous duelling ground. Nos. 13-14 built 1792 by Sir John Soane. Nos 57-8 built 1730 by Henry Joynes. Nos. 59 & 60 built 1640 by Inigo Jones. *OPEN 10.00-17.00 Tue-Sat. CLOSED B. hols.*

London's Wall

Surviving parts of the Roman and medieval wall around the old city of London can still be seen at St Alphage on the north side of London Wall EC1; St Giles Churchyard; Cripplegate EC1; Jewry St EC3; off Trinity Sq EC3 and in the Tower of London.

Mansion House   **6 N 30**

Opposite Bank of England EC2. 01-626 2500. Official residence of the Lord Mayor. Palladian building by George Dance 1739. Completed 1752. *OPEN Mon-Thur appt only.* Parties limited to 30.

Marlborough House   **5 K 19**

Marlborough Gate, Pall Mall SW1. 01-839 3411. Designed by Wren 1710. Contains a painted ceiling by Genti Peschi which was originally designed for the Queen's House at Greenwich. The simple classical-style Queen's Chapel in the grounds is by Inigo Jones, 1626. *Not open to the public.*

Old Bailey   **6 L 28**

Old Bailey EC4. 01-248 3277. The Central Criminal Court. On the site of old Newgate Prison. *Trials open to the public. Gallery OPEN 10.30-13.00 & 14.00-16.00 Mon-Fri. Minimum age 14. Free.*

Old Curiosity Shop   **6 J 25**

13-14 Portsmouth St WC2. 01-405 9891. Tudor style house now an antique and souvenir shop, believed to be the origin of Dickens' *'Old Curiosity Shop'. OPEN Mon-Sun Apr-Oct 09.00-17.30; Nov-Mar 09.30-17.30. Free.*

Old Palace

Old Palace Rd, Croydon, Surrey. 01-688 2027. Seat of the Archbishop of Canterbury for 1,000 years. Tudor chapel. *OPEN various afternoons during the year, 14.00-17.30. Conducted tours. Charge.*

Prince Henry's Rooms   **6 K 26**

17 Fleet St EC4. 01-353 7323. From 1610; oldest domestic building in London. Named after the son of James I. Fine plaster ceiling and carved oak panelling. *OPEN 13.45-17.00 Mon-Fri, 13.45-16.30 Sat. Small charge.*

Roman Bath   **6 K 24**

5 Strand La WC2. Disputed origin, restored in the 17th C. Not open but visible from the pathway.

Royal Exchange   6 N 31
Corner of Threadneedle St and Cornhill EC3. 01-606 2433. Built in 1884 by Tite. The third building on this site. Originally founded as a market for merchants and craftsmen in 1564, and destroyed in the Great Fire. The second building was also burnt down in 1838. Ambulatory containing statues and mural painting and courtyard.

Royal Mews   5 K 16
Buckingham Palace Rd SW1. Quadrangular design, built 1824-5. The Queen's horses and carriages, including the Coronation coach. *OPEN 14.00-16.00 Wed & Thur. CLOSED Royal Ascot week. Small charge.*

Royal Opera Arcade   5 J 21
Between Pall Mall and Charles II St SW1. John Nash 1816, London's earliest arcade. Pure Regency; bow-fronted shops, glass domed vaults and elegant lamps.

Skinners Hall   6 O 29
8 Dowgate Hill EC4. 01-236 5629. 17th-18th C buildings and quiet arcaded courtyard.

Smithfield EC1   6 K 29
Once 'Smooth Field'. Historical site of tournaments, public executions, cattle market and the famous Bartholomew Fair. In north east corner original Tudor gatehouse built over 13th C archway leading to Church of St Bartholomew the Great (see 'Churches'). South east side occupied by St Bartholomew's Hospital, London's oldest hospital, founded in 1123. Gateway (1702) bears London's only statue of Henry VIII. Smithfield Market is the largest meat market in the world (10 acres). The Italianate-style market buildings with some ornamental ironwork were designed by Horace Jones and erected between 1868 and 1899.

Somerset House   6 K 24
Strand WC2. 01-438 6622. On the site of an

unfinished 16th C palace. By Sir W. Chambers 1776. Used to house the register of births, marriages and deaths in England and Wales, now holds the Registry of divorce, wills and probate and the Inland Revenue.

St James's Palace   **5 K 19**

Pall Mall SW1. Built by Henry VIII with many later additions. Still officially a Royal residence. Ceiling of Chapel Royal by Holbein. *No admission to palace. Entry to courtyards only.*

Stock Exchange   **6 N 31**

Old Broad St EC2. 01-588 2355. Entrance to public gallery at corner of Threadneedle St and Old Broad St, showing the turmoil of 2,000 soberly dressed members milling below. Films shown in adjoining cinema. *Gallery OPEN 09.45-15.15 Mon-Fri. Last tour begins 14.30. Free. Parties up to 40, ring or write to PR Dept.*

The Temple   **6 L 26**

Inner Temple, Crown Office Row EC4. 01-353 8462. Middle Temple, Middle Temple La EC4. 01-353 4355. Both are Inns of Court. Enter by the gatehouse, 1685, in Middle Temple La. An extensive area of courtyards, alleys, gardens and warm brick buildings. Middle Temple Hall 1570. The Temple Church is an early Gothic 'round church' built by the Templars. 12th-13th C. *Inner Temple OPEN 10.00-16.00 Mon-Fri. CLOSED weekends, B. hols & legal vacations. Middle Temple Hall OPEN 10.00-11.30 & 15.00-16.00 Mon-Fri, 10.00-16.00 Sat. CLOSED Sun, B. hols & during examinations.*

Temple of Mithras, Bucklesbury House   **6 N 30**

Queen Victoria St EC4. Originally found 18 ft underground in Walbrook and moved here with other Roman relics.

The Tower of London   **6 Q 32**

Tower Hill EC3. 01-709 0765. A keep, a prison and still a fortress. Famous for the Bloody Tower, Traitors' Gate, the ravens, Crown Jewels and the Yeoman warders. Norman Chapel of St John. *Museum OPEN Mar-Oct 09.30-17.00 Mon-Sat, 14.00-17.00 Sun; Nov-Feb 09.30-16.00 Mon-Sat. Charge. Jewel House OPEN Mar-Oct 09.30-17.00 Mon-Sat, 14.00-17.00 Sun; Nov-Feb 09.30-16.00 Mon-Sat. Charge.*

World War 2 Operational Headquarters   **5 L 21**

Whitehall SW1. 01-233 8904 (08.30-09.30 only). A 6-acre honeycomb of rooms and corridors in the heart of government Whitehall, originally the secret war headquarters of Churchill's cabinet. War-time furnishings. *No longer open by appointment, but will be open to visitors as a museum Autumn 1983.*

York Watergate   5 K 22

Watergate Wlk, off Villiers St WC2. Built in 1626 by Nicholas Stone as the watergate to York House, it marks the position of the north bank of the Thames before the construction of the Victoria Embankment in 1862. The arms and motto are those of the Villiers family.

Whitehall

Wide thoroughfare used for ceremonial and State processions; contains the Cenotaph and several notable statues. Lined with Government offices.

Old Admiralty

1725-8 by T. Ripley. Fine Robert Adam columnar screen 1760. The New Admiralty 1887 lies behind.

Old Scotland Yard

1888. An asymmetrical building by Shaw.

The War Office

1898-1907. William Young. Victorian-baroque.

The Horse Guards

1750-60. William Kent.

Horse Guards

Banqueting House

Banqueting House

01-930 4179. 1619-25 17th C Palladian style by Inigo Jones built of Portland stone. Rubens ceilings 1630 were designed for Charles I. Changing of the Guard in the forecourt daily — see 'Daily ceremonies'. *OPEN 10.00-17.00 Tue-Sat, 14.00-17.00 Sun. CLOSED Mon except B. hols.*

Dover House

1755-8 by Paine. Entrance screen and rotunda 1787 by Henry Holland.

The Treasury

1846 Sir C. Barry. Victorian columned façade on Whitehall. Earlier façade overlooking Horse Guards Parade 1733-6 by William Kent.

The Foreign Office

Mid Victorian palazzo style by Gilbert Scott. Completed by Ministry of Housing 1920.

London bridges

The tidal Thames has 17 bridges. Noteworthy ones are:

Albert Bridge   **4 N 8**
Unusual rigid chain suspension. Built by Ordish 1875.

Chelsea Bridge   **5 P 12**
Original 1858. Rebuilt as suspension bridge by G. Topham Forrest & E. P. Wheeler in 1934.

London Bridge   **6 P 29**
The site of many replacements. Wooden construction until 13th C; the famous stone bridge that followed carried houses and shops. Granite bridge built in 1832 by Rennie was shipped off to Lake Havasu City, Arizona in 1971. Latest construction completed 1973.

Tower Bridge   **6 R 31**
Victorian-Gothic towers with hydraulic twin drawbridge. Jones and Wolfe Barry 1894. Breathtaking views of London and the Thames from the walkways. Also a museum housing the original Victorian steam engines. *OPEN Apr-Oct 10.00-18.30 Mon-Sun; Nov-Mar 10.00-16.45 Mon-Sun. CLOSED B. hols. Charge.*

Waterloo Bridge   **6 L 24**
Concrete. Fine design by Sir Giles Gilbert Scott 1940-5.

Westminster Bridge   **5 N 21**
Graceful cast iron. Thomas Page 1862.

Historic ships

Greenwich: The 'Cutty Sark'
King William Wlk SE10. 01-858 3445. Stands in dry dock. One of the great sailing tea-clippers, built 1869. 'Gipsy Moth IV', the boat in which Chichester sailed round the world in 1966 stands in dry dock next to the 'Cutty Sark'. *Both ships OPEN Apr-Sept 11.00-18.00 Mon-Sat, 14.30-18.00 Sun; Oct-Mar 11.00-17.00 Mon-Sat, 14.30-17.00 Sun. Charge.*

HMS Belfast   **6 R 31**
Symon's Wharf, Vine La SE1. 01-407 6434. Last surviving cruiser from World War II, moored near Tower Bridge. Explore bridge, decks, gun turrets, sick bay, galleys and engine rooms. Cross gangplank from Symon's Wharf, or by ferry from Tower Pier. *OPEN 11.00-17.55 Mon-Sun summer, 11.00-16.00 winter. Charge.*

RRS 'Discovery'   **6 R 33**
Historic Ships Collection, St Katharine's Dock E1.

01-481 0043. Captain Scott's 1901-4 Antarctica
vessel. Scott relics. *OPEN 10.00-17.00.*

Monuments and statues

*London has some 1,700 outdoor statues, memorials
and pieces of historic sculpture. Their subjects
range from classical mythology to modern states-
men. From such a number it is only possible to
suggest a selection of some of the best and most
interesting, which are listed below.*

Achilles   **2 I 16**
Hyde Pk W1. Westmacott, 1822. Erected to honour
Wellington. London's first nude statue.

Admiralty Arch   **5 K 21**
Entrance to the Mall SW1. Massive Edwardian triple
arch by Sir Aston Webb 1911. A memorial to Queen
Victoria.

Albert Memorial   **1 F 10**
Kensington Gore SW7. Statue of Prince Albert on a
memorial to the Great Exhibition of 1851, by Sir
George Gilbert Scott 1872.

Boadicea   **5 N 21**
Westminster Bridge SW1. Thornycroft, 1902.
Famous group showing the ancient British Queen
with her daughters in her war chariot.

The Cenotaph   **5 L 21**
Whitehall SW1. Designed 1920 by Sir Edward
Lutyens to honour the dead of World War I.

Charles I   **5 K 21**
Trafalgar Sq SW1. Le Sueur, 1633. The oldest
equestrian statue in London, and one of the finest.
Ordered to be destroyed during the Civil War and
hidden until the Restoration. It was erected on its
present site between 1675 and 1677.

Cleopatra's Needle   **6 L 23**
Victoria Embankment SW1. From Heliopolis. 1500
BC. Presented by Egypt and set up by the Thames
1878.

Eros   **2 I 20**
Piccadilly Circus W1. Gilbert, 1833. Officially the
Angel of Christian Charity. It is part of the memorial
to the Victorian philanthropist Lord Shaftesbury.
Made in aluminium.

George IV   **5 K 21**
Trafalgar Sq WC2. Chantrey, 1843. Rides without
boots on a horse without saddle or stirrups. Was
originally intended for the top of Marble Arch.

The Monument   **6 O 30**
Monument St EC3. A 17th C hollow fluted column
by Wren to commemorate the Great Fire of London.

Magnificent view. *OPEN Mar-Sept 09.00-17.40 Mon-Sat, 14.00-17.40 Sun; Oct-Mar 09.00-16.00 Mon-Sat. Charge.*

Nelson's Column 5 K 21
Trafalgar Sq SW1. 145-ft high column by William Railton 1840. Weighs 16 tons. At the top a statue of Nelson by Baily 1843.

Peter Pan 2 D 12
Kensington Gdns W2. Frampton, 1912. Charming fairy figure. Erected overnight as a surprise for the children.

Queen Elizabeth I 6 K 26
St Dunstan in the West, Fleet St EC4. Originally stood over Lud Gate. Made during the Queen's lifetime in 1586, it is one of London's oldest statues.

Royal Artillery Memorial 2 I 16
Hyde Pk Corner SW1. Jagger, 1925. London's best war memorial, with its great stone howitzer aimed at the Somme where the men it commemorates lost their lives. The bronze figures of soldiers are possibly the finest sculptures to be seen in London.

Victoria Memorial 5 K 17
In front of Buckingham Palace SW1. Brock, 1911. Impressive memorial to Queen Victoria which includes a fine dignified figure of the Queen, the best of the many statues of her.

Duke of Wellington 2 I 16
Hyde Pk Corner SW1. Boehm, 1888. Equestrian statue of the Duke. The memorial is distinguished by four well-modelled figures of soldiers in full kit. The Duke rides his favourite horse 'Copenhagen' and he looks towards Apsley House, in which he lived.

Whittington Stone
Highgate Hill N6, near junction with Dartmouth Pk Hill. Milestone marking the spot where tradition says young Dick Whittington rested on his way home from London and heard Bow Bells ring out, 'Turn again Whittington, thrice Lord Mayor of London', and returned to become London's most famous Mayor.

Houses of famous people

As you walk round London, look out for the round blue plaques, which you will see here and there on the sides of houses in historic parts of town. There are now over 450 of them, commemorating important events in the lives of the famous.

Carlyle's house   **4 M 8**
24 Cheyne Row SW3. 01-352 7087. A modest 18th C house where Carlyle lived for 42 years until his death in 1881. Portraits and manuscripts are among the memorabilia. *OPEN 11.00-17.00 Wed-Sat, 14.00-17.00 Sun. CLOSED Nov-Mar. Charge.*

Dickens' house   **3 G 27**
48 Doughty St WC1. 01-405 2127. Late 18th C terrace house. Relics of Dickens' life and writings. He lived here from 1837 to 1839. *OPEN 10.00-17.00. CLOSED Sun and B. hols. Charge.*

Hogarth's house
Hogarth La, Gt West Rd W4. 01-994 6757. The 17th C country villa of William Hogarth; relics and late impressions of his engravings. *OPEN 11.00-18.00 Mon-Sat, 14.00-18.00 Sun. CLOSED Tue and at 16.00 rest of week Oct-Mar. Free.*

Dr Johnson's house   **6 K 27**
17 Gough Sq, Fleet St EC4. 17th C house. Relics and contemporary portraits. He lived here from 1748 to 1759. *OPEN Mon-Sat May-Sept 11.00-17.30, Oct-Apr 11.00-17.00. CLOSED Sun & B. hols. Small charge.*

Keats' house
Wentworth Pl, Keats Gro NW3. 01-435 2062. The poet lived here during his prolific period 1818-20. *OPEN 10.00-13.00 & 14.00-18.00 Mon-Sat, 14.00-17.00 Sun. Free.*

Wellington Museum   **2 I 16**
Apsley House, 149 Piccadilly W1. 01-499 5676. Known as 'No. 1 London'. Duke of Wellington's house. Built 1771-8 from designs by Robert Adam and altered 1828 by B. D. Wyatt. Contains Wellington relics, fine Spanish (Velasquez) and Dutch paintings, silver plate and porcelain. *OPEN 10.00-17.50 Tue-Thur & Sat, 14.30-17.50 Sun. Small charge.*

Wesley's house & chapel   **6 K 33**
47 City Rd EC1. 01-253 2262. John Wesley's possessions and personal relics. His tomb is in the chapel grounds. *OPEN 10.00-16.00 Mon-Sat, 12.00-15.00 Sun. Small charge.*

Churches

London's churches fared badly in both the 'Great Fire' of 1666 and the blitz of World War 2. Yet those remaining, restored or rebuilt, are not only surprisingly numerous but form a remarkably fine collection well worth visiting. Here are some of the most interesting.

Abbeys and cathedrals
St Paul's Cathedral   **6 M 28**
EC4. 01-248 4619/2705. Wren's greatest work; built 1675-1710 replacing the previous church destroyed by the Great Fire. Superb dome, porches and funerary monuments. Contains magnificent stalls by Grinling Gibbons. Ironwork by Tijou, paintings by Thornhill and mosaics by Salviati and Stephens. *OPEN Apr-Sept 08.00-18.00; Oct-Mar 08.00-17.00. Crypt & galleries OPEN 10.00-16.15 Mon, Wed, Fri; 11.00-17.00 Tue, Thur & Sat all year.*

Southwark Cathedral   **6 Q 27**
Borough High St SE1. 01-407 2939. Much restored. Built by Augustinian Canons 1206. Beautiful early English choir and retrochoir. Tower built c. 1520, nave by Blomfield 1894-97. Contains work by Comper (altar screen).

Westminster Abbey   **5 M 20**
(The Collegiate Church of St Peter in Westminster) Broad Sanctuary SW1. 01-222 5152. Original church by Edward the Confessor 1065. Rebuilding commenced by Henry III in 1245 who was largely influenced by the new French cathedrals. Completed by Henry Yevele and others 1376-1506 (towers incomplete and finished by Hawksmoor 1734). Henry VII Chapel added 1503; fine perpendicular with wonderful fan vaulting. The Abbey contains the Coronation Chair, and many tombs and memorials of the Kings and Queens of England and their subjects. Starting place for pilgrimage to Canterbury Cathedral. *Royal Chapels OPEN 09.20-16.00 (last tickets) Mon-Fri, 09.20-14.00 & 16.00-17.00 Sat. Charge. 18.00-20.00 Wed (photography permitted) free. Museum OPEN Apr-Sept 09.15-17.00 Mon-Sat; Oct-Mar 09.15-15.30. Small charge.*

Westminster Roman Catholic Cathedral 5 M 16
Ashley Pl SW1. 01-834 7452. Early Christian Byzantine-style church by J. F. Bentley, 1903. The most important Roman Catholic church in England. Fine marbled interior.

Churches
Brompton Oratory   **1 I 11**
Brompton Rd SW7. 01-589 4811. Large Italian

Renaissance-style church designed by H. Gribble, 1884. Fine marbled interior and original statues from the Cathedral of Siena.

Chapel Royal of St John   **6 Q 32**

White Tower, Tower of London EC3. The oldest church in London, c. 1085, original Norman.

Holy Trinity   **5 L 12**

Sloane St SW1. By Sedding in 1890. London's most elaborate church of the 'Arts and Crafts' movement.

The Queen's Chapel, St James's Palace 5 K 19

Marlborough Rd SW1. Built by Inigo Jones 1623. Fine restored woodwork and coffered ceiling. *OPEN on application to the Administrative Officer, Marlborough House, SW1.*

St Bartholomew-the-Great   **6 K 29**

West Smithfield EC1. 01-606 5171. Norman choir of Augustinian Priory 1123 with later Lady Chapel; the only pre-Reformation font in the City. Tomb of founder who also founded St Bartholomew's Hospital; other fine monuments.

St Clement Danes   **6 K 25**

Strand WC2. 01-242 8282. First built for the Danes, 9th C. Spire by Gibbs. Rebuilt by Wren 1681. Destroyed in air raids 1941 and rebuilt and re-dedicated in 1958 as the central church of the RAF. Bells ring 'Oranges and Lemons' every 3 hrs. Fine moulded plaster roof.

St Martin-in-the-Fields   **5 K 22**

Trafalgar Sq WC2. 01-930 1862. James Gibbs, 1726. Famous spire and portico. Fine venetian east window and white and gold moulded plaster ceiling. Lunchtime music *13.00-14.00 Mon & Tue.*

St Paul's Covent Garden   **6 J 23**

Covent Garden WC2. 01-836 5221. Fine 'ecclesiastical barn' by Inigo Jones. Rebuilt by T. Hardwick after fire of 1795. Pleasant gardens at western (entrance) end.

St Peter-upon-Cornhill   **6 N 31**

Bishopsgate Corner EC3. 01-626 9483. Very fine church by Wren, 1677-87. Oldest church site in City, reputedly AD 179. Famous for Elizabethan music: organ built by Schmidt. Fine carved screen. 14th and 15th C plays performed at Xmas.

St Stephen Walbrook   **6 N 30**

Walbrook EC4. 01-626 2277. Masterpiece by Wren, 1672-79; steeple 1714-17. Dome, with eight arches, supported by Corinthian pillars, all beautifully restored. Fine fittings. Glass by Keith New. Lord Mayor of London's church and the home since 1953 of 'The Samaritans' set up to help the suicidal and desperate.

The great museums and galleries

London's national museums and galleries contain some of the richest treasures in the world. Apart from the museums owned by the nation, London is further enriched by other collections open to the public. Most were started as specialist collections of wealthy men or associations but are now available to all, by right or courtesy.

British Museum and Reference Library   3 G 24
Gt Russell St WC1. 01-636 1555. One of the largest and greatest museums in the world. Contains famous collections of Egyptian, Assyrian, Greek and Roman, British, Oriental and Asian antiquities. Among many outstanding and unique items are the Egyptian mummies, the colossal Assyrian bulls and lions in the Nimrud gallery. Cambodian and Chinese collections, the Elgin Marbles and the Rosetta Stone. Building 1823-47 by Sir Robert Smirke; the domed reading room 1857 is by Sidney Smirke. *OPEN 10.00-17.00 Mon-Sat, 14.30-18.00 Sun. Films Tue-Fri. Lectures Tue-Sat. Free.*

Courtauld Institute Galleries   3 F 24
Woburn Sq WC1. 01-580 1015. The Courtauld Collection of French Impressionists (including fine paintings by Cézanne, Van Gogh, Gauguin) and the Lee, Gambier-Parry and Fry Collections. *OPEN 10.00-17.00 Mon-Sat, 14.00-17.00 Sun. Charge.*

Geological Museum   1 H 10
Exhibition Rd SW7. 01-589 3444. Physical and economic geology and mineralogy of the world; regional geology of Britain. Models, dioramas and a large collection of gems, stones and fossils. *OPEN 10.00-18.00 Mon-Sat, 14.30-18.00 Sun. Free.*

Hayward Gallery   6 M 23
Belvedere Rd SE1. 01-928 3144. Changing exhibitions of major works of art arranged by the Arts Council. Fine modern building and river setting. *OPEN 10.00-20.00 Mon-Thur, 10.00-18.00 Fri & Sat, 12.00-18.00 Sun. Charge.*

Imperial War Museum   6 Q 23
Lambeth Rd SE1. 01-735 8922. Very popular national museum of all aspects of war since 1914. Collection of models, weapons, paintings, relics. The building was once a lunatic asylum. *Film shows 15.00 Sat & Sun. OPEN 10.00-17.50 Mon-Sat, 14.00-17.50 Sun. Free.*

London Transport Museum   **6 J 23**
Flower Market, Covent Gdn WC2. 01-379 6344. Story of London's transport. Historic road and rail vehicles, working exhibits and audio visual displays. *OPEN Mon-Sun 10.00-18.00. Charge.*

Madame Tussaud's   **2 B 19**
Marylebone Rd NW1. 01-935 6861. Waxworks effigies of the famous and notorious. New Chamber of Horrors created 1980. 'Battle of Trafalgar': reconstruction of gun-deck of 'Victory' at height of battle. *OPEN Mon-Sun Apr-Sept 10.00-18.00; Oct-Mar 10.00-17.30. Charge.*

Museum of London   **6 L 30**
London Wall EC2. 01-600 3699. Combined collections of the former London Museum and Guildhall Museum with extra material. A 3-dimensional biography of the City and London area, with models, reconstructions and even the Lord Mayor's Coach. *OPEN 10.00-18.00 Tue-Sat, 14.00-18.00 Sun.*

Museum of Mankind   **2 I 19**
6 Burlington Gdns W1. 01-437 2224. Exciting collection of primitives, including the Benin bronzes. *Film shows 11.30, 14.30 Tue-Fri. Opening times as the British Museum.*

National Gallery   **5 J 21**
Trafalgar Sq WC2. 01-839 3321. Very fine representative collection of the various schools of painting. Includes many world famous pictures. Rich in early Italian (Leonardo da Vinci, Raphael, Botticelli and Titian). Dutch and Flemish (Rembrandt, Rubens, Frans Hals, Van Dyck), Spanish 15-18th C

(Velasquez and El Greco), British 18th and 19th C (Constable, Turner, Gainsborough and Reynolds). Building 1838 by W. Wilkins. *OPEN 10.00-18.00 Mon-Sat, 14.00-18.00 Sun. Free.* Guided tours at *11.30 & 15.30 Mon-Fri.*

National Portrait Gallery   **5 J 22**
2 St Martin's Pl WC2. 01-930 1552. Historical collection of contemporary portraits of famous British men and women from early 9th C to the

present day. Excellent reference section of engravings and photographs. *OPEN 10.00-17.00 Mon-Fri, 10.00-18.00 Sat, 14.00-18.00 Sun. CLOSED B. hols. Free.*

Natural History Museum 1 H 9

Cromwell Rd SW7. 01-589 6323. The national collections of zoology, entomology, palaeontology and botany. Particularly notable are the bird gallery, the 90-ft model blue whale and the great dinosaur models. Built 1881 by A. Waterhouse. *OPEN 10.00-18.00 Mon-Sat, 14.30-18.00 Sun. Free.*

Queen's Gallery 5 K 17

Buckingham Palace, Buckingham Palace Rd SW1. 01-930 4832. Pictures and works of art from all parts of the Royal collection. Exhibitions changed at intervals. *OPEN 11.00-17.00 Tue-Sat, 14.00-17.00 Sun. Charge.*

Science Museum 1 H 10

Exhibition Rd SW7. 01-589 3456. The history of science and its application to industry. A large collection of very fine engineering models, steam engines, motor cars, aeroplanes and all aspects of applied physics and chemistry. Instructive children's gallery. *OPEN 10.00-18.00 Mon-Sat, 14.30-18.00 Sun. CLOSED B. hols. Free lectures & films, or write for brochure. Free.*

Tate Gallery 5 P 18

Millbank SW1. 01-821 1313. Representative collections of British painting from the 16th C to the present day; fine examples of Blake, Turner, Hogarth, the pre-Raphaelites, Ben Nicolson, Spenser and Francis Bacon; sculpture by Moore, Hepworth. Also a particularly rich collection of foreign paintings and sculpture from 1880 to the present day, including paintings by Picasso, Chagall, Mondrian, Pollock, Lichtenstein, Degas, Marini and Giacometti. Built 1897 by Sidney H. J. Smith. *OPEN 10.00-18.00 Mon-Sat, 14.00-18.00 Sun. Film shows 12.00 & 16.00 Mon-Fri. Lectures at various times. Free.*

Tower of London, the Armouries   **6 Q 32**

Tower Hill EC3. 01-709 0765. The Crown Jewels (heavily guarded). Largest collection of armour and arms in Britain. 10-20th C. *OPEN 09.30-17.00 Mon-Sat (to 16.00 winter), 14.00-17.00 Sun. CLOSED Sun winter & B. hols. Charge.*

Victoria and Albert Museum   **1 H 10**

Cromwell Rd SW7. 01-589 6371. A museum of decorative art, comprising vast collections from all categories, countries and ages. Over 10 acres of museum! Each category is extensive and choice. It includes important collections of paintings, sculpture, graphics and typography, armour and weapons, carpets, ceramics, clocks, costumes, fabrics, furniture, jewellery, metalwork and musical instruments. Fine Art collections include Sandby, Girtin, Cotman, Constable, Turner and some Raphael cartoons. The Prints and Drawings Dept has extensive collections dealing with art, architecture, pure and applied design, graphics, typography and craft. Also worth a visit is the Boilerhouse (01-581 5273) housing exhibitions dedicated to modern industrial design. *OPEN 10.00-17.50 Mon-Thur & Sat, 14.30-17.50 Sun. CLOSED Fri, B. hols. Free lectures at various times. Free.*

Wallace Collection   **2 D 18**

Hertford House, Manchester Sq W1. 01-935 0687. A private collection of outstanding works of art which was bequeathed to the nation by Lady Wallace in 1897. Splendid representation of the French 17th and 18th C, including many paintings by Boucher, Watteau and Fragonard. There are also several Rembrandts, a Titian, some Rubens, and paintings by Canaletto and Guardi. Important collections of French furniture. Sèvres porcelain, Majolica, Limoges enamel and armour. Also a fine collection of Bonnington oils and watercolours. *OPEN 10.00-17.00 Mon-Sat, 14.00-17.00 Sun. CLOSED B. hols. Free.*

Westminster Abbey Treasures   **5 M 20**

The Cloisters, Westminster Abbey SW1. 01-222 5152. Contains the famous wax effigies of British monarchs. Also plans, paintings, prints, and documents. *OPEN 10.15-16.00 Mon-Sat. Small charge.*

Whitechapel Art Gallery

80 Whitechapel High St E1. 01-377 0107. Frequent public exhibitions of great interest. The Whitechapel has successfully introduced new ideas in modern art into London. *OPEN 11.00-17.50 Sun-Fri. Free.*

The Royal parks

London is particularly rich in parks, gardens, commons, forests and heathland. There are over 80 parks within 7 miles of Piccadilly. The Royal parks are still the property of the Crown and were usually the grounds of Royal homes or palaces.

Greenwich Park SE10
01-858 2608. A Royal park of 200 acres with pleasant avenues lined with chestnut trees, sloping down to the Thames. Impressive views of the river, the shipping and the two classical buildings; the Queen's House by Inigo Jones and the Royal Naval College (once a Tudor Royal Palace). Contains also the old Royal Observatory and its pleasant garden. 13 acres of wooded deer park, a bird sanctuary and Bronze-age tumuli. *OPEN 07.00-21.15 summer, 07.00-18.00 or dusk winter.*

Hampton Court & Bushy Park, Middx
01-977 1328. 1,100 acres of Royal park bounded on two sides by the Thames. Hampton is the formal park of a great Tudor palace with ancient courts, superb flower gardens, the famous maze and the 'great vine' planted during Queen Anne's reign. Bushy Park is natural farmland, artificial plantation, watercress and ponds. Both parks have many fine avenues including the mile-long Chestnut Avenue with 'Diana' fountain in Bushy Park. Hampton Court itself is described under 'Getting Out'. *OPEN 07.45-dusk.*

Hyde Park W1   2 E 16
01-262 5484. A Royal park since 1536, it was once part of the forest reserved by Henry VIII for hunting wild boar and bulls. Queen Elizabeth I held military reviews here (still held on special occasions). It was the haunt of highwaymen until 1750 and even today is patrolled at night by police. The Great Exhibition of 1851 designed by Paxton was held opposite Prince of Wales Gate. Hyde Park now has 340 acres of parkland, walks, Rotten Row with horse-riders, and the Serpentine — a fine natural lake for fishing, boating and swimming. The Serpentine Bridge is by George Rennie, 1826. The famous 'Speaker's Corner' is near Marble Arch — public executions were held at Tyburn gallows nearby until 1783. Good open-air bar and restaurant overlooking the lake (near the bridge). *OPEN 12.00-22.30. No cars after dusk. The Lido OPEN May-Sept & hols 10.00-18.30 for swimming. Small charge.*

Kensington Gardens W8   1 D 10
01-937 4848. A formal and elegant addition to Hyde

Park. 275 acres of Royal park containing William III's lovely Kensington Palace, Queen Anne's Orangery, the peaceful 'Sunken Garden' nearby, the Round Pond with its busy model sailing-boats, and, on the south side, the magnificently Victorian 'Albert Memorial'. The famous Broad Walk, until recently flanked by ancient elms is now replanted with fragrant limes and maples and the nearby 'Flower Walk' is the home of wild birds, woodpeckers, fly-catchers and tree-creepers. Queen Caroline produced both the Long Water (Peter Pan's statue is here) and the Serpentine by damming the West-bourne river. Good children's playground. *OPEN 07.30-16.00*

Regent's Park NW1   **2 B 21**
01-935 1537. A Royal park of 470 acres, it was originally part of Henry VIII's great hunting forest in the 16th C. The Prince Regent in 1811 planned to connect the park (and a new palace) via the newly built Regent Street to Carlton House. Although never fully completed the design by John Nash (1812-26) is of great distinction, the park being surrounded by handsome Regency terraces and imposing gateways. Contains the zoo, the Regent's canal, a fine boating lake with 30 species of birds and the Queen Mary's rose garden within Nash's Inner Circle. Open-air threatre. *OPEN 05.00-dusk.*

Richmond Park, Surrey
01-940 0654. A Royal park of 2,500 acres first enclosed as a hunting ground by Charles I in 1637. Retains all the qualities of a great English feudal estate — a natural open park of spinneys and plantations, bracken and ancient oaks (survivors of the great oak forests of the Middle Ages) and over 600 red and fallow deer. Badgers, weasels and the occasional fox can be seen. *OPEN Mar-Sept 07.00-dusk; 07.30-dusk winter.*

St James's Park & Green Park SW1   **5 K 18**
01-930 1793. The oldest Royal park, acquired in 1532 by Henry VIII, laid out in imitation 'Versailles' style by Charles II, finally redesigned in the grand manner for George IV by John Nash in the 1820s. A most attractive park, with fine promenades and walks, and a romantic Chinese-style lake, bridge, and weeping willows. The bird sanctuary on Duck Island has some magnificent pelicans and over 20 species of ducks and geese. Good views of Bucking-ham Palace, the grand sweep of Carlton Terrace, the domes and spires of Whitehall and to the south, Westminster Abbey. The Mall and Constitution Hill are frequently part of ceremonial royal occasions. *OPEN 05.00-24.00.*

Zoos and aquaria

The London Zoo   2 A 21

Regent's Pk NW1. 01-722 3333. This famous zoo has one of the largest collections of animals in the world. Excellent aviary designed by Lord Snowdon and a 'Moonlight Hall' where day and night are reversed and rarely seen nocturnal animals are awake. The zoo was originally laid out by Decimus Burton in 1827; since then many famous architects have designed special animal houses. First class children's zoo. *OPEN 09.00-dusk; Nov-Feb 10.00-16.00, 09.00-19.00 Sun & B. hols. Charge.*

The London Zoo Aquarium   2 A 21

Regent's Pk NW1. 01-722 3333. Marine and Tropical Halls. Excellently lit and displayed. A well-stocked aquarium of both sea and freshwater fish and amphibians from European and tropical waters. Particularly notable are the sea fish, the octopus, stingrays and sharks. *OPEN 09.00-dusk; Nov-Feb 10.00-17.30, 09.00-19.00 Sun & B. hols. Charge.*

Longleat Lion Reserve

Warminster, Wilts. Maiden Bradley 328. Visitors to the magnificent Renaissance house can choose to drive through the game park where lions roam at will! You can  stop your car and watch in safety but it is extremely foolhardy to get out, however friendly the lions. Also has a chimpanzee island. No soft-topped cars allowed. *OPEN 10.00-dusk. Charge.*

Whipsnade Park Zoo

Dunstable, Beds. Whipsnade 872171. A 500-acre 'natural' zoo of woods and downland in the Chilterns. 2,000 animals in large open-air enclosures. Some species roam freely throughout the park. You can picnic in the grounds — take binoculars or use the telescopes provided. Travel within the park in your own car or by miniature motor-coach train. London 35 miles (M1). *OPEN 10.00-19.00 or dusk. Charge.*

Windsor Safari Park

Winkfield Rd, Windsor, Berks. Windsor 69841. Drive round the park in the car (long queues in summer). Lion and baboon reserves, monkey jungle, zebra, camels, giraffes, and lakes with waterfowl and a reptile house. Dolphins give hourly performances in the Dolphinarium. *OPEN 10.00-dusk. Charge.*

L👀king at London

London from the water
Trips on the Thames
During the summer months daily services run from the following piers:
Charing Cross
Victoria Embankment WC2. 01-839 5320. Trips to the Tower *approx every ½ hr;* to Greenwich *every 45 mins.* Also evening cruises at *19.30.*
Tower Pier
Tower Hill EC3. 01-709 9697. Trips to Greenwich *approx every 25 mins;* to Westminster *every 25 mins. Ferry to HMS Belfast when open.*
Westminster Pier
Victoria Embankment SW1. 01-839 2349. Trips to the Tower *every 20 mins;* to Greenwich *approx every 20 mins;* to Kew *every ½ hr;* three services a day to Hampton Court and Richmond.

Trips on the canal
Jason's Trip
Opposite 60 Blomfield Rd W9. 01-286 3428. The traditional narrow boat 'Jason' leaves Little Venice for 1½ hr return trip, with commentary, through Regent's Park and Zoo to Camden Lock. Refreshments and lunch available. *Depart Jun-Aug 10.30, 12.30, 14.30, 16.30; May-Sept 12.30, 14.30, 16.30; Easter-mid Oct 14.30, 16.30.* Evening trips (groups only) *depart 19.30.*
Jenny Wren Cruises
250 Camden High St NW1. 01-485 4433. 1½ hr round trips along Regent's Canal passing the zoo and Little Venice. Up to 4 tours a day *daily from Easter to end Sept.* Also longer and evening trips.
Zoo Water Bus
British Waterways Board, Delamere Ter W2. 01-286 6101. Boat leaves from the end of Delamere Ter for ½ hr trip to the zoo. *Apr-Sept daily 10.00-16.45 (Sun & B. hols till 17.55). Last return boat leaves zoo 17.25 (Sun & B. hols till 18.30).* Visit to the zoo optional.

Viewpoints

A nice way of orientating oneself or seeing London with a fresh sense of alignment is to go to the top of one of the very tall, new buildings. Together with old favourites and natural viewpoints, these are the most outstanding.

Alexandra Palace
On Muswell Hill N22. About 250 ft. View from the park over Kent, Surrey, Essex and Hertfordshire.

Hampstead Heath NW3
450 ft high. Constable's famous view of London. A more comfortable view from:

Jack Straw's Castle
North End Way NW3. 01-435 8885. Lunch and dinner in the restaurant with long views across London to the distant Kentish hills. *CLOSES 23.00 LD (Sun traditional L only).*

Kenwood House NW3
Panorama of almost the whole of London. View from the gazebo by the coach house.

London Hilton   **2 I 16**
Park La W1. 01-493 8000. Roof bar at 320 ft. Lift. Fine views on Hyde Park, Buckingham Palace and Mayfair.

The Monument   **6 O 30**
Monument St EC3. Magnificent view from the top, but it is 202 ft high and you have to climb the stairs. *OPEN Mar-Sept 09.00-17.40 Mon-Sat, 14.00-17.40 Sun; Oct-Mar 09.00-16.00 Mon-Sat. Small charge.*

St Paul's Cathedral EC4   **6 M 28**
Magnificent view of the City, the Wren churches, the Tower and London Pool. 335 ft. 727 steps. *OPEN Mon-Fri 10.00-16.15, Sat 11.00-16.15 summer; open to 15.15 winter. CLOSED Sun. Charge.*

Tower Bridge   **6 R 32**
Excellent river views from the walkways.

Daily ceremonies

These are the main ceremonies which occur throughout the year. Phone the London Tourist Board information (01-730 0791) or Leisureline (01-246 8041) for details of daily events.

Ceremony of the Keys   **6 Q 32**
Tower of London EC3. The Chief Warder of the Yeoman Warders, with an escort of the Brigade of Guards, locks the West Gates, the Middle Tower and Byward Tower. One of the oldest military ceremonies in the world. *Mon-Sun 21.40, by written*

application to the Governor well in advance, enclosing sae.

Changing of the Guard   5 K 17
Buckingham Palace SW1. Takes place inside the palace railings and in summer the crowd makes it impossible to see much. An alternative is to see the Guards on their way from Chelsea or Wellington Barracks; phone the LTB to find out which they are leaving from on the day you are going. *Mon-Sun in summer, alternate days in winter.* Leave Chelsea Barracks at *10.45* or Wellington Barracks at *11.00.* Palace ceremony *11.30.*

St James's Palace SW1   5 K 19
A detachment of the Buckingham Palace Guard comes here. Guards change *11.15 (days as above).*

Whitehall SW1   5 L 21
Horse Guards Pde SW1. Changing of the Queen's Life Guard mounted on splendid black horses. Guards leave Hyde Park Barracks *10.38 Mon-Sat, 09.39 Sun.* Ceremony *11.00 Mon-Sat, 10.00 Sun.*

Seasonal events in London

The following list presents not only the most important annual events but also some of the more obscure London customs in order to cover as wide a field as possible. For exact days, times and places, where not given, contact one of the centres given under 'Information centres'.

Spring

Chelsea Flower Show   4 N 11
Royal Hospital Grounds, Chelsea SW3. 01-730 7036. Superb flower displays. *For 3 days late May. No fixed date.*

Chinese New Year   2 I 22
Soho, Gerrard St W1. Papier-mâché dragon and lit-up festivities march through the centre of London's Chinese community. *Jan or Feb.*

Cruft's Dog Show   1 H 4
Earls Court, Warwick Rd SW5. 01-385 1200. *Early Feb.*

Easter Procession & Carols   5 N 20
Westminster Abbey SW1. 01-222 5152. *Easter Mon.*

Easter Sunday Parade   4 P 9
Battersea Park SW11. Colourful carnival procession preceded by a parade of old vehicles. *Easter Sun.*

FA Cup Final
Empire Stadium, Wembley, Middx. 01-902 1234. The climax of the English football season. *2nd Sat in May.*

London Harness Horse Parade   2 A 21
Regent's Park NW1. Fine horses and carts; brewers' vans and drays on parade. Judging *starts at 09.45* followed by a procession twice round the Inner Circle *at about 12.00. Easter Mon.*

May Day   2 I 15
Labour Party procession to Hyde Park. *1st Mon May.*

Oxford v Cambridge Boat Race
River Thames, Putney to Mortlake. University boat race over four miles. View from the banks of the river or one of the bridges. Get there early for a good view. Race *begins 14.00, Sat in Marh or Apr.*

Putney & Hammersmith Amateur Regattas
01-748 3632. Rowing regattas make exciting watching from the river banks.

Royal Film Performance
A selected film gets royal patronage in aid of charity. Celebrities and glitter at one of the big cinemas. *No fixed date.*

Rugby League Challenge Cup Final
Wembley, Middx. *1st Sat in May.*

Spring Antiques Fair   4 L 9
Chelsea Old Town Hall, Kings Rd SW3. 01-352 2263. *Mid Mar.*

Summer Art Exhibition   2 I 18
Royal Academy, Burlington House, Piccadilly W1. 01-734 9052. *May–mid-Aug.*

Summer
All England Lawn Tennis Championships
All England Lawn Tennis & Croquet Club, Church Rd, Wimbledon SW19. 01-946 2244. 'Wimbledon Fortnight', the world's most famous championship. *Last week Jun & 1st week Jul.*

Bank Holiday Fair
Hampstead Heath (nr North End Way) NW3. *Aug B. hol Mon.*

Doggetts Coat & Badge Race
The Thames, London Bridge to Chelsea. 01-626 3531. Rowing race for Thames Watermen, originated in 1715. Sometimes called the 'Watermen's Derby'. *Late Jul.*

Election of Sheriffs of the City of London
Guildhall EC2. 01-606 3030. Lord Mayor and Aldermen in a colourful ceremony. Posies are carried traditionally to ward off 'the plague'. *24th Jun.*

Fine Art & Antiques Fair   1 C 3
Olympia, Hammersmith Rd W14. 01-603 3344. *Early Jun.*

The Garter Ceremony

Service, attended by the Queen at St George's Chapel, Windsor, preceded by a colourful procession with the Household Cavalry and Yeomen of the Guard. Ceremony dates from 14th C. *Mon afternoon of Ascot week (usually third week in Jun).*

Lord's Test Match

Lord's Cricket Ground, St John's Wood Rd NW8. Tickets 01-289 1615. Prospects of play 01-286 8011. *Jun or Jul.*

Proms

(Henry Wood Promenade Concerts)   1 F 10

Royal Albert Hall, Kensington Gore SW7. 01-589 8212. Concerts of classical music. Tickets by ballot only for first and last nights. *Late Jul until Sept. No fixed date.*

Royal Ascot Races

A fashionable society event where hats attract more attention than the horses. *Jun.*

Royal International Horse Show

Empire Pool, Wembley, Middx. 01-902 1234. Top-class show jumping competition in the presence of Royalty. *Mid Jul. No fixed date.*

Royal Tournament   1 H 4

Earls Court, Warwick Rd SW5. 01-385 1200. Impressive military spectacle with marching displays and massed brass bands. *Mid Jul 2 weeks. No fixed date.*

Royal Tournament March Past   5 L 21

Horse Guards, Whitehall SW1. Colourful parade by all 'troops taking part in the Royal Tournament. *15.00 Sun before Tournament.*

Trooping the Colour   5 L 21

The route is from Buckingham Palace SW1 along the Mall to Horse Guards Parade, Whitehall and back again. Pageantry at its best for the Queen's official birthday. *11.00, Sat nearest 11th Jun.*

Autumn

Battle of Britain Week   5 N 20

Thanksgiving service at Westminster Abbey SW1. 01-222 1051. Biggin Hill Flying Display where veteran aircraft are on show. *Early Sept.*

Costermongers' Harvest Festival   5 K 22

St Martin-in-the-Fields, Trafalgar Sq WC2. 01-930 1862. Service attended by the 'Pearly Kings and Queens', in their colourful regalia. *15.30, 1st Sun in Oct.*

Harvest of the Sea Thanksgiving   6 P 31

St Mary at Hill, Lovat La EC3. 01-626 4184. Also a

fine display of fish at the church. *11.00, 2nd Sun in Oct.*

Horse of the Year Show
Wembley Stadium, Empire Way, Wembley, Middx. 01-902 1234. Fine show jumping. *Early Oct.*

Winter

Admission of the Lord Mayor Elect
The Lord Mayor takes office. Colourful ceremony at Guildhall including handing over of insignia by former Lord Mayor. *Fri before Lord Mayor's show.*

Guy Fawkes Day
Anniversary of the Gunpowder Plot of 1605. Private and public firework displays. *Evening, 5th Nov.*

London to Brighton Veteran Car Run   2 I 16
Hyde Park Corner W1. Cars leave here for Brighton. Colourful event with contestants in period costume. Commemorates the anniversary of Emancipation Day. *08.00 1st Sun Nov.*

Lord Mayor's Procession & Show
The newly elected Lord Mayor is driven in his state coach from the Guildhall to the Law Courts to be received by the Lord Chief Justice. The biggest ceremonial event in the City. *2nd Sat Nov.*

New Year's Eve   5 K 21
Trafalgar Sq WC2. Singing of 'Auld Lang Syne' by massed crowds also dancing around (sometimes in) the fountains.

Remembrance Sunday   5 L 21
Poppies sold in the streets to raise money for ex-servicemen. Service at the Cenotaph, Whitehall SW1 with a salute of guns. *11.00 2nd Sun Nov.*

Royal Command Performance   3 E 27
Usually at London Palladium, Argyll St WC1. 01-437 7373. Variety show in aid of charity occasionally attended by the Queen. *No fixed date.*

St Paul's Cathedral EC4   6 M 28
Watchnight service *22.00-24.00. 31st Dec.*

State Opening of Parliament   5 N 20
The Queen, in the Irish state coach, is driven from Buckingham Palace to the House of Lords. A royal salute is fired from St James's Park. *Early Nov. No fixed date.*

Tower of London Church Parades   6 Q 32
Tower of London EC3. The Yeoman warders in state dress are inspected and parade before and after morning service on the *Sun before Xmas 11.00. Also Easter Sun & Whit Sun.*

Westminster Carol Service   5 M 20
Carol services on *26th, 27th and 28th Dec.*

LONDON NIGHTLIFE

Night clubs

London's top night clubs are expensive, but the facilities they offer are good; membership (M) is usually necessary for entry. You can only enter a gaming house as a member or a guest of a member. By law, when you join a gaming club, you will not be admitted until you have filled in a declaration of your intent to gamble and 48 hrs has elapsed from this time. Membership charges vary considerably. The number 48 after the club's entry means that the 48 hr rule applies.

Bristol Suite   **2 H 18**
14 Bruton Pl W1. 01-499 1938. Hostesses, music and an international cuisine. *D OPEN 22.00-03.30 Mon-Fri*. A. Ax. B. Dc. **£££.**

Clermont   **2 H 18**
44 Berkeley Sq W1. 01-493 5587. Excellent restaurant and wine list. **£££ (48).**

Golden Nugget   **2 I 21**
22-32 Shaftesbury Av W1. 01-734 6211. Meals served in bar. **£ (48).**

Office   **2 G 19**
16 Avery Row W1. 01-499 6728. Discreet private club with dancing to a pianist and recorded music. Hostesses. (M) reduced for visitors. *OPEN to 03.30. CLOSED Sat & Sun*. Cabaret *24.00*. A. Ax. B. Cb. Dc. **££.**

Penthouse   **2 I 17**
11 Whitehorse St W1. 01-493 1977. *OPEN 18.30-03.00. CLOSED Sun & Mon*. (M). **££.**

Riots   **4 P 5**
5-13 Battersea High St SW11. 01-223 9777. Stylish and popular nightspot with a conservatory restaurant. Dazzlingly lit dance floor. *OPEN to 01.15. CLOSED Sun*. (M). A. Ax. B. Dc. **£££.**

Stork Club   **2 I 20**
99 Regent St W1. 01-734 1393. Plush newish club with lots of red velvet. Luxury restaurant serving French cuisine. Dance band. Singers and dancers *from 22.00. Spectacular cabaret from Paris at 00.30. OPEN 20.30-03.30 Mon-Sat*. Dinner, supper and breakfast. **£££+.**

Discotheques and rock music

Discotheques generally cater for the affluent young, the new celebrities and the fashionable. They are very numerous; these are probably the best and most popular. Membership is often necessary. London is the hub of the rock music industry in Britain. The rock places listed here have live bands plus dancing and disco between performances.

Dingwall's
Camden Lock, Chalk Farm Rd NW1. 01-267 4967. Club by the Regent's canal which was once a stable for barge horses. Restaurant. Video. *OPEN 20.00-02.00 Mon-Sat. CLOSED Sun.* Drinks half price before *22.00*. Also free jazz sessions *12.00-15.00 Sat.*

Hombré de Bahia   **2 F 21**
78 Wells St W1. 01-580 2881. Live groups and disco. Buffet and three bars. *OPEN 21.00-03.30 weekdays (24.00 Sun).* **£.**

Le Kilt   **2 H 22**
60 Greek St W1. 01-734 9598. Lively disco, a long-time favourite of the French. *OPEN 20.00-03.00.* **£.**

Lyceum   **6 K 24**
Wellington St WC2. 01-836 3715. Large club which used to be a theatre. Disco *20.00-01.00 Fri, 20.00-02.00 Sat.* **££.**

Marquee   **2 I 21**
90 Wardour St W1. 01-437 6603. One of the original London rock clubs; concentrates mainly on heavy rock. Snacks. *OPEN 19.00-23.00 Mon-Sat, 19.00-22.30 Sun.*

Reflections   **2 B 14**
22 Praed St W2. 01-262 7952. Aptly named, this disco has mirrors everywhere. Spacious dance floor. Snacks. *OPEN Wed-Sat 21.30-02.00.* **£.**

Rock Garden   **6 J 23**
6-7 The Piazza, Covent Garden WC2. 01-240 3961. Restaurant. *OPEN 19.30-02.00 Mon-Thur, to 03.00 Fri & Sat, 19.30-24.00 Sun.*

Samantha's   **2 H 20**
3 New Burlington St W1. 01-734 6249. A well known and lively place with groups and discs. *OPEN 20.30-03.30 Mon-Sat. CLOSED Sun.* **£.**

Thursdays   **1 D 4**
38 Kensington High St W8. 01-937 7744. Popular non-membership club. Large complex includes 4 bars, a good dance floor and restaurant. Jeans banned. *OPEN 21.00-03.00 Mon-Sat.* **££.**

Upstairs at Ronnie's   **2 H 22**
47 Frith St W1. 01-439 0747. A separate club over
the famous jazz club. *OPEN 21.30-03.00 Mon-Sat.*

Whisky-A-Go Go   **2 I 21**
35 Wardour St W1. 01-437 5534. The 'grandaddy' of
discotheques. Resident DJ, bar, snacks and basket
meals. *OPEN 21.00-03.00. Sun to 01.00.* **£.**

Dinner dancing

*Differs from the previous section with the emphasis
on the food as opposed to the music, which is either
in a separate room or at a lower volume than in the
discotheques. No membership is necessary.*

Boulogne   **2 I 22**
27 Gerrard St W1. 01-437 3186. Formal atmosphere
with French food. Resident quartet and cabaret
nightly. *OPEN to 03.00. CLOSED Sun.* A. Ax. B. Dc.
££.

Entrecote   **3 G 25**
124 Southampton Row WC1. 01-405 1466/8640.
Wood panelled restaurant with a romantic candlelit
atmosphere. International cuisine though the
accent is French. Three-piece band and on *Sun* a
guitarist. *OPEN to 01.30.* A. Ax. B. Dc. **££.**

Foobert's   **2 G 20**
18 Foubert's Pl W1. 01-734 3630. Large and
modern, seats 200. Restaurant and small dance
floor. Three bars. Popular with young foreigners.
Disco *from 21.00. OPEN to 03.00 Mon-Sat.* Ax. B.
Cb. Dc. **££.**

L'Hirondelle   **2 I 20**
99-101 Regent St W1. Entrance in Swallow St.
01-734 6666. Theatre restaurant with two floorshows nightly. International menu. *OPEN
20.30-03.30. CLOSED Sun.* A. Ax. B. Cb. Dc. **£££.**

London Room   **3 I 24**
Drury La cnr Parker St WC2. 01-831 8863. Modern,
purpose-built theatre restaurant with tiered seating.
Dancing and cabaret. Well-known acts. Price
includes dinner and wine. *OPEN Mon-Sat
20.00-01.00.* A. Ax. B. Cb. Dc. **£££.**

Omar Khayyam   **2 H 20**
177 Regent St W1. 01-437 3000. Decorated in true
Sultan's style; opulent cabaret and authentic belly
dancers. Two bands and two floorshows nightly.
OPEN 21.00-03.00. CLOSED Sun. A. Ax. B. Dc. **£££.**

Roof Restaurant   **2 I 16**
Hilton Hotel, Park La W1. 01-493 8000. The view is

all you would imagine. Two bands. French food. *OPEN 19.30-02.00.* A. Ax. B. Dc. **£££.**

Savoy Restaurant   **6 K 23**
Savoy Hotel, Strand WC2. 01-836 4343. Elegant and formal with resident quartet. World famous reputation for classic cooking and service. *OPEN 19.30-02.00. Closed Sun.* A. Ax. B. Dc. **£££.**

Terrace Restaurant   **2 H 16**
Dorchester Hotel, Park La W1. 01-629 8888. Pleasant atmosphere. Live music, but no cabaret. Dancing from *22.00.* Dinner à la carte. *OPEN 18.00-01.00. CLOSED Sun.* A. Ax. B. Cb. Dc. **£££+.**

Tiddy Dol's   **2 I 16**
2 Hertford St W1. 01-499 2357. An 18th C house in Shepherd Market. Excellent game and English dishes with dancing in the music room and English entertainment every evening. *D OPEN to 02.00.* A. Ax. B. Cb. Dc. **£££+.**

Jazz clubs

100 Club   **2 G 22**
100 Oxford St W1. 01-636 0933. Lively, noisy, British jazz and room to dance. Bar and food. *Tue* punk, *Thur* reggae. Other nights jazz. *Mon* modern. *OPEN 19.30-24.00 Mon-Wed, 19.30-01.00 Thur-Sat, 19.30-23.00 Sun. Charge.*

Pizza Express   **2 H 22**
10 Dean St W1. 01-439 8722. Jazz sessions in the basement. *OPEN Tue-Sun 21.00-02.00. Charge.*

Ronnie Scott's   **2 H 22**
47 Frith St W1. 01-439 0747. The best jazz in London backed by the right blend of good food, comfort and subtle lighting. On the stand a succession of big name jazzmen, usually USA imports. *OPEN 20.30-02.00 Mon-Thur, to 03.00 Fri & Sat. CLOSED Sun. Charge.*

Stanhope   **1 I 7**
97 Gloucester Rd SW7. 01-373 4192. Jazz club in a pub. (M). *OPEN daily 20.30-22.45. Small initial charge for membership.*

Theatres, cinemas and music

London theatre is famous throughout the world for its diversity and quality with popular productions in the West End, subsidised quality at the National

Theatre and Royal Shakespeare and a lively fringe and experimental sector. See the weekly 'Time Out' for reviews of fringe and experimental theatre and evening papers and 'What's On in London' for lists of current cinema and theatre.

Opera, ballet and concert halls

Barbican Hall   **6 K 30**
Barbican Centre, Barbican EC2. 01-638 4141. New base for the London Symphony Orchestra who play here regularly. Visits by other orchestras, light entertainment and pop concerts. Superb architecture and design at this new arts Centre.

Coliseum   **5 J 22**
St Martin's La WC2. 01-836 3161. Largest London theatre seating 2,400. Now houses the resident English National Opera *Aug-May*, and visiting companies during summer months.

Covent Garden   **6 J 23**
Royal Opera House, Bow St WC2. 01-240 1066. Information and bookings 01-240 1911 (24-hr). The world-famous Royal Ballet and Royal Opera companies maintain an international reputation.

The Place   **3 D 25**
17 Duke's Rd WC1. 01-387 0161. Home of the London Contemporary Dance Theatre and the London School of Contemporary Dance, an exciting and creative modern dance company. Immaculate production with interesting choreographic ideas.

Royal Albert Hall   **1 F 10**
Kensington Gore SW7. 01-589 8212. Victorian domed hall named after Prince Albert, built 1871. Orchestral, choral, pop concerts and public meetings. Famous for the 'Proms'.

Royal Festival Hall   **6 M 23**
South Bank SE1. 01-928 3191. Built in 1951 for the Festival of Britain. Seats 3,000. Orchestral and choral concerts. Forms the South Bank Arts Centre with the Queen Elizabeth Hall, Purcell Room, National Film Theatre, and Hayward Gallery.

Sadler's Wells   **3 G 30**
Rosebery Av EC1. 01-837 1672. Once a spa (the original well discovered by Thomas Sadler is under a trap-door at the back of the stalls). Birthplace of the Royal Ballet Company and now used by visiting opera and dance companies.

Cinemas Tel. nos.
ABC 1 & 2 636 8861
Academy 1 437 2981
Academy 2 437 5129
Academy 3 437 8819
Astral 1 & 2 437 5839
Barbican 628 8795
Biograph 834 1624
Centa Charles Peggy 437 8339
Cinecenta 1 & 2 437 3561
Cinecenta 1,2,3 & 4, 930 0631
Classic (Oxford St.) 636 0310
Classic (Leicester Sq.) 930 6915
Classic (Haymarket) 839 1527
Classic 1,2 & 3 (Tott. Ct. Rd.)
636 6148
Classic 734 5414
Curzon 499 3737
Dominion 580 9562
Empire 437 1234
Eros 437 3839
Film Centa 9 & 3 437 4815
Gala Royal 262 2345
Gate Bloomsbury 837 8402
Gate New Oxford 493 20317
ICA 930 6393
Jacy 930 1143
Leicester Sq Theatre 930 5252
London 437 4555
Lumiere 836 0691
Minema 235 4225
Moulin 1, 2, 3, 4 & 5 437 1653
National Film Theatre 928 3232
Odeon (Haymarket) 930 2738
Odeon (Leicester Sq.) 930 6111
Odeon (Marble Arch) 723 2011
Odeon Shaftesbury Av. 836 0691
Plaza 1, 2, 3 & 4 437 1234
Prince Charles 437 8181
Rialto 437 3488
Scene 1, 2, 3 & 4 439 4470
Studio 1,2,3 & 4 437 3300
Warner West End 439 0791

Theatres Tel. nos.
Adelphi 836 7611
Albery 836 3878
Aldwych 836 6404
Ambassadors 836 1171
Apollo 437 2663
Arts 836 2132
Astoria 437 1801
Barbican 628 8795
Coliseum 836 3161
Comedy 930 2578
Covent Garden 240 1066
Criterion 930 3216
Drury Lane 836 8108
Duchess 836 8243
Duke of York's 836 5122
Fortune 836 2238
Garrick 836 4601
Globe 437 1592
Haymarket 930 9832
Her Majesty's 930 6606
ICA 930 6393
Jeannetta Cochrane 242 7040
Lyric 437 3686
May Fair 629 3036
Mermaid 236 5521
National Theatre 928 2252
New London 242 9802
Old Vic 928 7616
Palace 434 0834
Palladium 437 7373
Phoenix 836 2294
Piccadilly 437 4506
Players 839 1134
Prince Edward 437 6877
Prince of Wales 930 8681
Purcell Room 928 3191
Queen Elizabeth Hall 928 3191
Queen's 734 1166
Royal Albert Hall 589 8212
Royal Festival Hall 928 3191
Sadler's Wells 837 1672
St. Martin's 836 1443
Savoy 836 8888
Shaftesbury 836 6596
Strand 836 2660
Vaudeville 836 9988
Victoria Palace 834 1317
Warehouse 836 6808
Westminster 834 0283
Whitehall 930 6692
Wigmore Hall 935 2141
Wyndham's 836 3028
Young Vic 928 6363

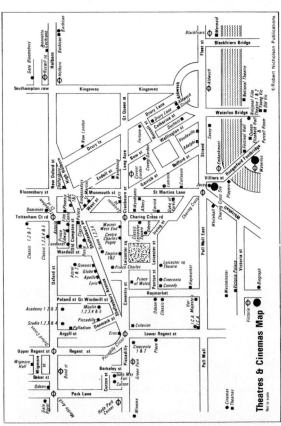

Theatres & Cinemas Map
Not to scale

© Robert Nicholson Publications

Restaurants

American

Also see 'Inexpensive eating'.

Drones   **5 J 12**
1 Pont St SW1. 01-235 9638. Stylishly spread over
two floors serving chicken, scampi, steak, fish,
selection of hamburgers, shakes and ices. *LD OPEN
to 24.00.* A. Ax. B. Dc. Children. **££.**

L. S. Grunt's   **6 J 23**
12 Maiden La WC2. 01-379 7722. Lively pizza hide-
out in converted electricity station. Wittily entitled
pizzas, salads, cocktails. *LD OPEN to 23.30.
CLOSED Sun.* **£.**

Maxwells
76 Heath St NW3. 01-794 5450. Eat country style
fried chicken and salads with a Hawaiian touch,
delicious sweets, all very good value. *LD OPEN to
24.00 Sun-Thur, to 01.00 Fri & Sat.* Children. **£.**

The Widow Applebaum's Deli and Bagel
Academy   **2 F 19**
46 South Molton St W1. 01-629 4649. American-
Jewish delicatessen with a lengthy menu offering
101 dishes. Chopped liver, matzo balls, good hot
pastrami, and a large selection of sandwiches,
salads, burgers, ice cream sodas and giant sundaes.
LD OPEN to 22.00. Sat to 18.00. CLOSED Sun. **£.**

Chinese: Cantonese

*The cooking of Canton and southern China. Nearly
all Chinese restaurants in this country are
Cantonese and nearly all have unfortunately made
many concessions to English taste. Cantonese
when authentic is very good indeed. It differs from
Pekingese mainly by being more liquid. It is
steamed, boiled or braised — herbs and sauces are
widely used.*

Chuen Cheng Ku   **2 I 21**
17 Wardour St W1. 01-734 3509. Unpretentious
and totally authentic restaurant, well patronised by
Chinese. Good fish dishes and excellent value

lunches. *LD OPEN all week to 24.00* A. Ax. B. Dc. **£.**

Good Friends
139 Salmon La E14. 01-987 5498. Chinese Cantonese restaurant in the Chinatown of Limehouse, near the docks. Has a high reputation. *LD Reserve. OPEN to 24.00.* A. Ax. B. Dc. **££.**

Lee Ho Fook　　　　　　　　　　　**2 I 22**
15 Gerrard St W1. 01-734 9578. Patronised by numerous Chinese for the good cooking and reasonable prices. Cantonese roast duck, sliced steak in black bean sauce, suckling pig. *LD Reserve. OPEN to 23.30.* A. Ax. B. Dc. **£.**

Poons
41 King St WC2. 01-240 1743.　　　　　**6 J 23**
27 Lisle St WC2. 01-437 1528.　　　　　**2 I 22**
Has a very good reputation. Extremely varied and large menu; wind-dried meats, pork belly, duck liver sausage. *LD Reserve D. OPEN to 23.30. CLOSED Sun.* Ax. Dc. **££.**

Chinese: Pekingese
The dishes of Peking, Formosa and northern China are considered to be the highest form of Chinese cuisine and often equal in quality to the best French cooking. The food is drier and sharper than Cantonese (often roasted or quick fried) and the 7 to 8 courses are all eaten separately as a 'banquet' – a leisurely ceremonial occasion ideally shared between 4 to 6 people. If possible order the day before – you can leave the choice to the restaurant. The great dishes are Peking duck and Mongolian hot-pot.

Mr Chow　　　　　　　　　　　　**2 H 13**
151 Knightsbridge SW1. 01-589 7347. Pekingese food, with Italian overtones. Modern décor and paintings. Peking duck, sole in wine. *LD Reserve. OPEN to 23.45.* A. Ax. B. Cb. Dc. **£££.**

Dumpling Inn　　　　　　　　　　**2 I 22**
15a Gerrard St W1. 01-437 2567. A Soho branch of Richmond. Rendezvous with similarly genuine Pekingese cooking. The place for 'food', but not an intimate chat. Crowded. Prawns in chilli sauce, beef in oyster sauce. *LD OPEN to 23.30.* Ax. B. Dc. **££.**

English
Many pubs also serve good lunches based on traditional English cooking. Refer to the section 'Pubs'.

Baker & Oven　　　　　　　　　　**2 C 19**
10 Paddington St W1. 01-935 5072. A restaurant in a converted Victorian bakery. Original bakers' ovens

still used to cook enormous portions of English food. Soups, pies, roasts and game, all very good. *LD Reserve. OPEN to 23.00. CLOSED Sun, L Sat.* A. Ax. B. Dc. Children. **££.**

Baron of Beef 6 M 29

Gutter La (off Gresham St) EC2. 01-606 6961. First-class variety of English food eaten in great comfort. Impeccable service. Roast Scotch beef, braised oxtail, steak and kidney pie, fresh fruit. *LD OPEN to 21.30. CLOSED Sat & Sun.* A. Ax. B. Dc. **££.**

Hungry Horse 4 K 7

196 Fulham Rd SW10. 01-352 7757. A mirrored ceiling, wooden tables and modern décor. English cooking at its best. Home-made soups, onion and anchovy salad, calves' brains, kedgeree. *D Reserve. OPEN to 24.00. (23.00 Sun). CLOSED L Sat.* A. B. Dc. **££.**

Lockets 5 O 18

Marsham Ct, Marsham St SW1. 01-834 9552. Richly panelled and dignified, popular with MPs from round the corner. Attractively presented English dishes. Lamb with juniper berries, spiced beef cooked in strong ale. Fine wine list. *LD OPEN to 23.00. CLOSED Sat & Sun.* A. Ax. B. Cb. Dc. **£££.**

Massey's Chop House 2 I 12

38 Beauchamp Pl SW3. 01-589 4856. Simple, pleasant old-style chop house. All meats charcoal grilled; home-made pâté. T-bone steak. *LD OPEN to 22.45. CLOSED Sun in winter.* A. Ax. B. Cb. Dc. **££.**

Rules 6 J 23

35 Maiden La, Strand WC2. 01-836 5314. Genuine Edwardian eating house with very good traditional English food. Jellied and smoked eels, grouse pie, duckling with orange sauce. *LD Reserve. OPEN to 23.15, Sat to 22.45. CLOSED Sun, L Sat.* A. Ax. B. Dc. **££.**

Simpson's-in-the-Strand 6 K 23

100 Strand WC2. 01-836 9112. A famous restaurant with an Edwardian club atmosphere. The attentive service and the large carvings from enormous joints of beef and lamb are the best feature. Draught beer. *LD Reserve. OPEN to 22.00. CLOSED Sun.* A. B. **£££.**

Wiltons 5 J 19

27 Bury St SW1. 01-930 8391. Small, distinguished and Edwardian with art nouveau décor. Simple and delicious English food. Oysters, lobsters and excellent game. *LD OPEN to 22.15. CLOSED Sat & Sun, D Fri.* Ax. Dc. **£££+.**

French

The following all serve classical French cooking at its best. Some specialise in simple French provincial dishes, others in highly sophisticated cuisine.

Ark

122 Palace Gdns Ter W8. 01-229 4024. | **1 C** | **8** |
35 Kensington High St W8. 01-937 4294. | **1 E** | **8** |

Good French provincial food. Onion soup, noisette d'agneau, foie de veau. *LD OPEN to 23.30. CLOSED Sun L.* Ax. B. **££.**

Bagatelle   **4 L   5**

5 Langton St SW10. 01-351 4185. Relaxed atmosphere with friendly and efficient service. Duck pâté, fillet of sole, tarte aux pommes. *D Reserve. OPEN to 23.00. CLOSED Sun.* A. Ax. B. Dc. **££.**

Berkeley Hotel Restaurant   **2 I 14**

Wilton Pl SW1. 01-235 6000. French cuisine of consistent excellence in strikingly decorated room. Many of the dishes are the chef's variations on classical themes. Old-fashioned formal service. *LD Reserve. OPEN to 22.45. CLOSED Sat.* A. B. **£££.**

Bubbs   **6 K 29**

329 Central Market EC1. 01-236 2435. Pleasant restaurant near Smithfield meat market. Menu changes often, splendid desserts. *L Reserve. OPEN to 14.00. CLOSED Sat & Sun.* **££.**

Capital Hotel Restaurant   **2 I 13**

22-24 Basil St SW3. 01-589 5171. Small, conveniently situated hotel with first class French cuisine. Quenelles de Brochet à l'Americain carré d'agneau aux herbes, sorbet au fine Champagne. *LD Reserve. OPEN to 22.30.* A. Ax. B. Cb. Dc. **£££.**

L'Etoile   **2 F 22**

30 Charlotte St W1. 01-636 7189. Typically French in atmosphere and style. Top-quality food and attentive service. Caldeirada, rognons sautés au vin rouge, turbot à la Monégasque. Better at lunch. *LD Reserve. OPEN to 22.00. CLOSED Sat & Sun.* **£££.**

Le Gavroche   **2 F 16**

43 Upper Brook St W1. 01-408 0881. Luxury restaurant with haute cuisine. Soufflé suissesse, caneton Gavroche, omelette soufflé Rothschild. Cooking variable but service faultless. *D Reserve. OPEN to 23.15. CLOSED Sat & Sun.* A. Ax. Cb. Dc. **£££+.**

Au Jardin des Gourmets   **2 H 22**

5 Greek St W1. 01-437 1816. Unassuming but impeccable French classical cuisine. Good wines. *LD Reserve. OPEN to 23.30. CLOSED Sun, L Sat.* A. Ax. B. Dc. **££.**

Langan's Brasserie   **2 I 19**
Stratton St W1. 01-493 6437. Vast L-shaped room seating 200. Popular and very trendy. Small menu, erratic service. *LD Reserve. OPEN to 23.00. CLOSED Sun, L Sat.* Ax. Dc. Children. **££.**

Mon Plaisir   **3 I 23**
21 Monmouth St WC2. 01-836 7243. Small, spartan, typically French bistro. Unobsequious but friendly service. Saumon en papillote, escalope à la crème, entrecôte Mon Plaisir. *LD Reserve. OPEN to 23.00. CLOSED Sat L & Sun.* **££.**

La Poule au Pôt   **5 L 14**
231 Ebury St SW1 01-730 7763. Casual and friendly, with reasonable prices. Ratatouille, carbonnade de boeuf lapin aux deux moutardes. *LD Reserve. OPEN to 23.15. CLOSED Sun.* A. Ax. B. **££.**

German and Austrian
Kerzernstuberl   **2 E 18**
9 St Christopher's Pl W1. 01-486 3196. Authentic Austrian food and music on the accordion, with yodelling. You are expected to join in, so be prepared for a noisy evening. *D Reserve. OPEN to 23.00. CLOSED Sun & Sat L.* A. Ax. B. Dc. Children. **££.**

Old Vienna   **2 G 19**
94 New Bond St W1. 01-629 8716. Gay Austrian atmosphere, music and excellent cooking. Rindsbraten sacherart, paprika Huhn Franz Lehar, sachertorte. *LD OPEN to 00.30. CLOSED Sun & L Sat.* A. Ax. B. Dc. **££.**

Tiroler Hut
27 Westbourne Gro W2. 01-727 3981. Tyrolean atmosphere; waitresses in national dress. Dancing, yodelling. Good value, excellent cooking. Leberknodel suppe, jagerschnitzel and apfel strudel. *D OPEN to 24.00. CLOSED Mon.* A. Ax. B. Dc. **££.**

Greek and Turkish
Many Greek restaurants are run by Cypriots who have absorbed the best of both Greek and Turkish dishes into their style of cooking.
Adana Kebab Centre
17 Colomb St SE10. 01-858 1913. Busy Turkish restaurant with excellent Mediterranean foods; chicken with lemon and bay leaves. Retsina or buzbag to drink. *D Reserve. OPEN to 24.00. CLOSED Sun.* Dc. **£.**

Beotys   **5 J 22**
79 St Martin's La WC2. 01-836 8768. Comfortable

establishment with authentic Greek cooking. Taramasalata, dolmadakia, arnaki. *OPEN to 23.30. CLOSED Sun.* A. Ax. B. Dc. **££.**

Chagalayan Kebab House
86 Brent St NW4. 01-202 8575. Well prepared food appetisingly presented; charcoaled kebabs, lamb on the bone (kleftiko), moussaka, salads. *LD Reserve Sat & Sun. OPEN to 24.00. CLOSED L Sun.* A. Ax. B. Dc. **£.**

Cypriana Kebab House   2 G 22
11 Rathbone St W1. 01-636 1057. Greek Cypriot food. Pleasant and not too expensive. Friendly service. Specialities range from talatouri salad to sheftalia. *OPEN to 23.30. CLOSED Sun, L Sat.* B. Dc. Children. **£.**

Kalamaras Taverna   1 A 11
76 Inverness Mews W2. 01-727 9122. True taverna atmosphere. Bouzouki players on some evenings. Superb national dishes ranging from xolmades to baklava. *D Reserve. OPEN to 24.00. CLOSED Sun.* A. Ax. B. Dc. Children. **££.**

White Tower   2 G 22
1 Percy St W1. 01-636 8141. Elegant; first class cuisine. Agreeable and leisurely service. Lemon soup, moussaka, dolmades. *LD Reserve. OPEN to 22.30. CLOSED Sat & Sun.* A. Ax. B. Dc. **£££.**

Hungarian
Hungarian food is distinguished by unusual but extremely tasty dishes. Fish are all of the freshwater variety. Carp and pike are presented in an impeccable style.

Gay Hussar   2 H 22
2 Greek St W1. 01-437 0973. Much-loved by the media. Excellent Hungarian cooking. Good, enthusiastic service. Cold wild cherry soup, bulgar salata, roast partridge with lentils. *LD Reserve. OPEN to 22.45. CLOSED Sun & B. hols.* **££.**

Le Mignon   1 A 11
2 Queensway W2. 01-229 0093. Typical Hungarian food, cheerful atmosphere and live gipsy orchestra. House sulz, chicken hongroise, fantanyeros. *LD OPEN to 24.00.* A. Ax. B. Dc. Children. **££.**

Indian
The farther south in India the hotter the spices. Madras, Bendi and Vindaloo mean climbing degrees of heat. For the European however there is no particular virtue in an excess of hotness — many Indians also enjoy (and prefer) mild curries. Hindu

cooking uses vegetables in rich liquid juices; Muslims use more meat and the food is drier. The best cooking uses the traditional clay oven and adds spices individually to each dish, giving a distinctive and piquant flavour.

Diwan-I-Am   **2 E 22**
161 Whitfield St W1. 01-387 0293. Tandoori restaurant which is deceptively large due to a system of 'caves' downstairs. Chicken and prawn tandoori dishes, Indian sweets. *LD Reserve D. OPEN to 24.00.* A. Ax. B. Dc. **£.**

Holy Cow   **1 C 8**
38c Kensington Church St W8. 01-937 2005. North Indian curries. Tandoori dishes. Cocktail bar. *LD Reserve. OPEN to 23.45.* A. Ax. Dc. B. **££.**

Rama Sita   **1 A 5**
6 Clarendon Rd W11. 01-727 9359. Recreates ancient recipes little known in the West. The accent is on herbs rather than spices. *LD Reserve. OPEN to 23.00. CLOSED Sun.* **££.**

Star of India   **1 I 7**
154 Old Brompton Rd SW5. 01-373 2901. Excellent Indian food and good service. Mughlai dishes must be ordered in advance. Prawn biriani, kebab. *LD OPEN to 24.00. Sun to 23.30.* A. Ax. B. Dc. **£.**

Veeraswamy's   **2 I 20**
99-101 Regent St (entrance in Swallow St) W1. 01-734 1401. Authentic food in 'Indian Empire' atmosphere. Moglai, Delhi, Madras, Ceylon and Vindaloo curries. *LD OPEN to 23.30 (Sun 22.00).* A. Ax. B. Cb. Dc. **££.**

International
Borshtch N'Tears
45 Beauchamp Pl SW3. 01-589 5003.   **2 I 12**
273 Kings Rd SW3. 01-352 5786.   **4 L 4**
Loud, musical and very popular. Slav restaurant. Unofficial dancing and much cheer. Large menu —boeuf strogonoff, chicken Kiev, lamb kebabs in vast portions. Advisable to arrive before 20.00 or after 22.00. *D Reserve for parties over 7. OPEN to 01.30.* A. Ax. B. Dc. **£.**

Carrier's   **3 E 32**
2 Camden Pas N1. 01-226 5353. Owned by the gourmet Robert Carrier. Eat in either a French 19th C inn or a Gothic greenhouse in the garden. Classic dishes from the famous cook book: lamb in Greek pastry, roulade of red caviar, petit pôt au chocolat à l'orange. Table d'hôte only. *LD Reserve. OPEN to 23.30. CLOSED Sun.* A. Ax. B. Dc. **£££+.**

Connaught Hotel
2 G 17

Carlos Pl W1. 01-499 7070. Smooth, discreet and unchanged. Panelled dining room or à la carte grill. Mainly English and French cuisine. Oeufs en surprise Connaught, silverside of beef, tournedos cendrillon. *LD OPEN to 22.00. Grill CLOSED Sat & Sun. Reserve.* A. **£££+.**

Daphne's
4 K 11

112 Draycott Av SW3. 01-589 4257. Small and dimly lit. Theatrical clientele. Very good soups. Roast grouse, veau au romarin. *D Reserve. OPEN to 24.00. CLOSED Sun.* A. Ax. B. Dc. **£££.**

Inigo Jones
5 J 22

14 Garrick St WC2. 01-836 6456. Extremely popular restaurant in a former workshop for making stained glass, samples of which are on display. First-rate food on a regularly-changed menu: smoked salmon and sour cream blinis, carré d'agneau, plus many seasonal dishes. *LD Reserve. OPEN to 23.45. CLOSED Sat L & Sun.* A. Ax. B. Dc. **£££.**

Ivy
2 I 22

1-5 West St WC2. 01-836 4751. Old established, first-rate restaurant, popular with theatrical personalities. Deep velvet chairs and period paintings enhance its restfulness. Confident cooking, using fresh ingredients; a mixture of Italian and French dishes. Good value set meal. Excellent wine list. *LD Reserve. OPEN to 23.00. CLOSED Sun, L Sat.* A. Ax. B. Cb. Dc. **££.**

Leith's
1 A 8

92 Kensington Pk Rd W11. 01-229 4481. Tastefully offbeat décor in this converted private house complements the originality of the menu. Preparation, presentation and service are excellent. Leith's duckling, trout mousse, ginger syllabub. *D Reserve. OPEN to 24.00, Sun to 23.15.* A. Ax. B. Dc. **£££+.**

Mirabelle
2 I 17

56 Curzon St W1. 01-499 4636. A famous Mayfair restaurant, renowned for fine cooking and a magnificent wine cellar. Homard Mirabelle, aiguillettes de canetons aux truffles. Must book. *LD Reserve. OPEN to 23.00. CLOSED Sun & B. hols.* A. Ax. B. Dc. **£££+.**

Italian
Bertorelli's
2 F 22

19 Charlotte St W1. 01-636 4174. Busy straightforward Italian eating places. Good food at reasonable prices. Scampi, veal cutlet royal, filets de sole Bertorelli, zabaglioni. Courteous and attentive

service. *LD OPEN to 22.00. CLOSED Sun & B. hols.*
Children. **££.**

Biagi's   **2 D 16**

39 Upper Berkeley St W1. 01-723 0394. Well run,
intimate small trattoria with fishing décor.
Good varied Italian dishes. Scaloppine alla crema, entrecote alla pizzaiola, saltimbocca. *LD Reserve. OPEN
to 23.00.* A. Ax. B. Cb. Dc. **££.**

La Capannina   **2 I 22**

24 Romilly St W1. 01-437 2473. Popular typical
Soho trattoria. Music in the evening. Petto di pollo,
vitello alla pianni. *LD Reserve. OPEN to 23.30.
CLOSED Sun & L Sat.* Ax. B. Dc. **££.**

Gondoliere   **1 F   8**

3 Gloucester Rd SW7. 01-584 8062. Food served by
Venetian gondoliers. Welcoming, restful atmosphere. Authentic cooking. Cartoccio del gondoliere,
dover sole del gondoliere. *LD OPEN to 23.00.
CLOSED Sun & L Sat.* A. B. **££.**

Hostaria Romana   **2 H 22**

70 Dean St W1. 01-734 2869. Boisterous and busy,
consistently good Roman cuisine. Regularly
changed menu. Crespoline alla Romana, agnellino
al forno, torta di mela. *LD Reserve. OPEN to 23.30.
CLOSED Sun.* A. Ax. B. Cb. Dc. Children. **£.**

Peter Mario   **2 I 22**

47 Gerrard St W1. 01-437 4170. Carefully cooked
food in a friendly setting. Generous helpings. Excellent soups, scaloppini Peter Mario. *LD OPEN to
23.15. CLOSED Sun.* A. Ax. B. Cb. Dc. Children. **££.**

San Frediano   **4 L   4**

62 Fulham Rd SW3. 01-584 8375. Bright and lively
trattoria with friendly service. Excellent Italian
dishes, particularly good fish and a tempting sweet
trolley, all at reasonable prices. Clam salad,
scallopino uccellato. *LD Reserve. OPEN to 23.15.
CLOSED Sun.* A. Ax. B. Dc. **££.**

San Lorenzo   **2 1 12**

22 Beauchamp Pl SW3. 01-584 1074. Very popular
and friendly restaurant offering a different menu
every day. *LD OPEN to 23.30. CLOSED Sun.* **££.**

Tiberio   **2 H 17**

22 Queen St W1. 01-629 3561. Top-quality Roman
cooking in popular, crowded atmosphere. Band for
dancing, *22.30-02.00.* Fettucine alla panna, duck
and quail. *LD Reserve. OPEN to 01.00. CLOSED
Sun & L Sat.* A. Ax. B. Cb. Dc. **£££.**

Verbanella

35 Blandford St W1. 01-935 2174	**2 D 18**	
145 Notting Hill Gate W11. 01-229 9882	**1 A 8**	

30 Beauchamp Pl SW3. 01-584 1107   **2 I 12**
Cheerful, efficient, popular and inexpensive; good cooking. Scaloppine alla Borromeo, petto di pollo alla Milanese. *D Reserve. OPEN to 23.30. CLOSED Sun*. A. Ax. B. Dc. Children. **££**.

Japanese
Hokkai   **2 I 21**
61 Brewer St W1. 01-734 5826. Japanese prints and red lanterns. Traditional dishes. *LD Reserve. OPEN to 22.45. CLOSED Sun L & Tue*. A. Ax. B. Dc. **££**.

Masako   **2 E 18**
6-8 St Christopher's Pl W1. 01-935 1579. The first authentic Japanese restaurant in London. Service by graceful and charming Japanese girls in kimonos. Completely oriental atmosphere where you can eat in true Japanese style. Try the complete dinner, Sukiyaki or Tempura. Saké or Japanese beer. *LD OPEN to 22.00. CLOSED Sun*. Ax. B. Cb. Dc. **££**.

Jewish
Bloom's
90 Whitechapel High St E1. 01-247 6001.
130 Golders Green Rd NW11. 01-455 1338.
Authentic Kosher restaurants. Busy and popular. Probably the best Jewish cooking in London. Large helpings: lockshen and meatballs, salt beef, stuffed kishka. *LD OPEN to 21.30. CLOSED Fri from 15.00, Sat & Jewish hols*. **£**.

Harry Morgan's
31 St John's Wood, High St NW8. 01-722 1869. All-Jewish menu care of Mrs Morgan. Very reasonable prices. Gefilte fish, latkes (sweet, fried, crisp potato pancakes). Hungarian goulash. *LD OPEN to 22.00, Fri to 15.00. CLOSED Mon*. **£**.

Russian
Luba's Bistro   **1 I 11**
6 Yeoman's Row SW3. 01-589 2950. Individual, down to earth, spartan atmosphere. Good peasant style cooking at low prices. Borscht, beef Stroganoff, shashlik, pojarsky. *LD OPEN to 23.30. CLOSED Sun*. Children. A. Ax. B. **£**.

Scandinavian
Hungry Viking   **1 B 9**
44 Ossington St W2. 01-727 3311. All the food here is home-made and includes pâtés, marinated herring and the traditional Smorgasbord. Good hot soup of the day. *D Reserve. OPEN to 23.30 Tue-Sat, to 23.00 Sun. CLOSED Mon*. A. Ax. B. Cb. Dc. Children. **£**.

Spanish and Mexican

El Bodegon   **4 L 6**
9 Park Wlk SW10. 01-352 1330. Intimate, cool and popular. Mainly Spanish dishes, excellently cooked. Gambas al pil-pil, paella, caneutos de carne. *LD OPEN to 24.00*. A. Ax. B. Cb. Dc. **££.**

La Cucaracha   **2 H 22**
12-13 Greek St W1. 01-734 2253. London's first Mexican restaurant, in the cellars of a converted monastery. Raw fish cocktail, arroz à la poblana, enchiladas. Spicy and delicious. *LD OPEN to 23.00. CLOSED Sun & Sat L*. A. Ax. B. Cb. Dc. **££.**

Martinez   **2 I 20**
25 Swallow St W1. 01-734 5066. Old-fashioned, beautifully decorated Spanish-style restaurant. Courteous service; guitarist. Gazpacho, a variety of paellas, good tortillas. *LD Reserve. OPEN to 23.15. CLOSED Sun*. A. Ax. B. Dc. **££.**

Valencia   **1 I 2**
1 Empress Approach, Lillie Rd SW6. 01-385 0039. Authentic, Spanish with singing waiters, guitarists, sherry on the house and flamenco on Sundays. Good seafoods and wines. *D Reserve. OPEN to 24.00*. **££.**

Swiss

The Swiss Centre   **2 I 22**
10 Wardour St (Leicester Sq) W1. 01-734 1291. Four different restaurants of varying prices, of which the Taverne seems the most popular. Imaginative decoration. Fondue, Swiss country hams, sausages and delicious pastries. *LD OPEN to 24.00*. A. Ax. B. Cb. Dc. **£–£££.**

Fish

As well as those restaurants, some of which are listed here, that specialise in elaborately cooked fish dishes, London has a large number of fish and chip 'take away' shops, mostly to be found in residential areas. Fish and chips is a national dish which you can take away soused with vinegar, salt and pepper. Eaten hot it can be delicious and good value. (The following restaurants are not fish and chip shops.)

Bentley's   **2 I 20**
11-15 Swallow St W1. 01-734 4756. Famous seafood restaurant and oyster bar. Lobster Newburg, sole menunière, prawns, fish of many sorts. *LD Reserve. OPEN to 22.30. CLOSED Sun*. A. Ax. B. Cb. Dc. **££.**

Manzi's   **2 I 22**
1-2 Leicester St WC2. 01-734 0224. Typical busy provincial Italian fish restaurant with bar. Street-

level room is best. Good swift service and cooking. Jellied eels, mussels, lobster and sole. *LD Reserve. OPEN to 23.30. CLOSED L Sun.* A. Ax. B. Cb. Dc. **££.**

Overton's   5 J 19
5 St James's St SW1. 01-839 3774. Long-established fish restaurant of character. 'Old world' atmosphere in the nicest sense. Oysters, lobsters, Dover sole. *LD Reserve. OPEN to 22.30. CLOSED Sun.* A. Ax. B. Dc. **£££.**

Le Suquet   4 K 11
104 Draycott Av SW3. 01-581 1785. French fish restaurant. Relaxed atmosphere with efficient and helpful service. *LD Reserve. OPEN to 23.15. CLOSED Mon & L Tue.* Ax. **£££.**

Sweeting's   6 N 29
39 Queen Victoria St EC2. 01-248 3062. Echo of a vanished age. Fish parlour, with excellent service. Sit at the bar and eat herrings with mustard, whitebait, fish pie of excellent quality. Good carafe and port. *L OPEN to 15.00. CLOSED Sat & Sun.* **££.**

Wheeler's fish restaurants
A group of restaurants specialising in expertly cooked fish dishes. Welcoming atmosphere with sophistication. Scallops, lobster Normande, sole Egyptian and shellfish.

Alcove   1 D 4
17 Kensington High St W8. 01-937 1443. As in all Wheeler's restaurants, only fresh ingredients of high quality are used in the preparation of fish dishes, whitebait, sole bonne femme, prawn thermidor. *LD Reserve. OPEN to 22.45. CLOSED Sun.* A. Ax. B. Cb. Dc. **£££.**

Antoine   2 F 22
40 Charlotte St W1. 01-636 2817. Small restaurant on 3 floors specialising in sea food. Lobster, smoked salmon, moules marinière and many ways of serving sole and halibut. *LD Reserve. OPEN to 23.00. CLOSED Sat.* A. Ax. Cb. Dc. **£££.**

Wheeler's   2 I 22
19 Old Compton St W1. 01-437 2706. *LD Reserve. OPEN to 22.45. CLOSED Sun.* A..Ax. B. Cb. Dc. **£££.**

Vegetarian and health food
Cranks   2 H 21
8 Marshall St W1. 01-437 9431. Also in Heals, Tottenham Court Rd. Modern, attractive décor; background of classical music. Home-made soups, hot vegetable savoury, mixed salads with fruit and nuts, good cheeses and sweets, and bread from their own bakery. *LD OPEN to 23.00; to 20.30 Mon. CLOSED Sun.* **££.**

Food for Thought   **3 I 23**

31 Neal St WC2. 01-836 0239. Vegetarian whole-food in a cheerful Covent Garden basement. Occasional 'music and poetry evenings'. *LD OPEN to 20.00. CLOSED Sat & Sun.* **£.**

Nuthouse   **2 H 20**

26 Kingly St W1. 01-437 9471. Buffet service vegetarian health food on two floors. Nut roasts, quiches, blackberry pie, fresh raspberry juice. *L OPEN to 19.00. Sat to 16.00. CLOSED Sun.* **£.**

Oodles

31 Cathedral Pl EC2. 01-248 2550/2559.	**6 M 28**
128 Edgware Rd W2. 01-723 7548.	**2 D 16**
3 Fetter La EC4. 01-353 1984.	**6 K 26**
113 High Holborn WC1. 01-405 3838.	**3 I 25**
42 New Oxford St WC1. 01-580 9521.	**3 H 24**

Very popular; clean scrubbed tables. Well-balanced salads and savoury foods. Generous hot dishes. *Opening times vary.* **£.**

Sharuna Restaurant   **3 H 23**

107 Gt Russell St WC1. 01-636 5922/3/4. An elegant South-Indian vegetarian restaurant. The highest quality and cleanliness. Vegetarian curries, delicately spiced, yogurt and fruit. *LD OPEN to 23.00 (Sun 21.00).* A. Ax. B. Dc. **£.**

Carveries

The carveries below are excellent value for money. The price includes a 3-course meal. Customers carve as much and as often as they like from enormous succulent joints of beef, lamb and pork.

Carvers' Corner   **6 N 30**

Buckler's Bury House, 18 Walbrook EC4. 01-248 4735. *L OPEN 11.30-15.00. CLOSED Sat & Sun.* A. Ax. B. Dc. **££.**

Cumberland Hotel   **2 E 16**

Marble Arch W1. 01-262 1234. *LD OPEN to 22.00.* A. Ax. B. Cb. Dc. **££.**

Piccadilly Hotel   **2 I 20**

Piccadilly W1. 01-734 8000. *LD OPEN to 22.00 Mon-Sat; to 21.30 Sun.* A. Ax. Cb. Dc. **££.**

Regent Palace Hotel   **2 I 20**

Piccadilly Circus W1. 01-734 7000. *LD OPEN to 21.00 Mon-Sat; to 18.00 Sun.* A. Ax. B. Cb. Dc. **££.**

Strand Palace Hotel   **6 K 23**

Strand WC2. 01-836 8080. *LD OPEN to 22.00.* A. Ax. B. Dc. **££.**

Westmoreland Hotel

18 Lodge Rd, St John's Wood NW8. 01-722 7722. *LD OPEN to 22.00.* A. Ax. Cb. Dc. **££.**

Inexpensive eating

Places where you can eat well for under £4.00. The café serving sausage, egg and chips is not included here, however excellent some may be. This list prizes distinctive or unusual cooking and atmosphere — but particularly good value for money.

Asterix   4 L 7
329 Kings Rd SW3. 01-352 3891. Large range of fillings in savoury and sweet crêpes. Normandy cider. Constant classical music. *LD OPEN to 24.00.*

Bistro Vino
1 Old Brompton Rd SW7. 01-589 3888.   **1 I   9**
303 Brompton Rd SW3. 01-589 7898.   **4 J 10**
5 Clareville St SW7. 01-373 3903.   **1 I   8**
2 Hollywood Rd SW10. 01-352 6439.   **4 K   6**
Started in 1958, this 'chain' shows no signs of breaking, judging by their fame for good simple bistro food at very reasonable prices in cheerful if noisy surroundings. *D OPEN to 23.45.* Children.

Ceylon Tea Centre   2 I 20
22 Regent St SW1. 01-930 8632. Good, varied and unusual salads, savouries and cheese flans. The different sorts of tea are first class. *L OPEN to 18.00. CLOSED Sun.*

Chicago Pizza Pie Factory   2 G 19
17 Hanover Sq W1. 01-629 2669. Crowded American restaurant with American style bar. Video tapes of Chicago football, baseball and hockey games. Serves 'big-shouldered' pizzas — more filling than other pizzas. *LD OPEN to 23.30. CLOSED Sun.*

Daquise   1 I 9
20 Thurloe St SW7. 01-589 6117. Simple, very cheap Polish food. Pierozki, shashlik, bitok. Many Polish customers. Also open for afternoon tea when they serve some of the most delicious pastries in London. *LD OPEN to 22.30.*

Geales   1 B 8
2 Farmer St W8. 01-727 7969. Large selection of excellent fish and chips; cod's roe, scampi, sole. Wine list. *LD OPEN to 22.45. CLOSED Sun & Mon.* A.

Hard Rock Café   2 I 16
150 Old Park La W1. 01-629 0382. One of the best hamburger places in London with relaxed, colourful atmosphere. Chequered tablecloths, wooden tables, rock music. A cocktail bar and good hamburgers, sandwiches and steaks. Schlitz beer. Expect a queue. *LD OPEN to 00.30.*

Jimmy's   2 H 22
23 Frith St W1. 01-437 9521. Popular Turkish basement restaurant, especially with students. Large

helpings of meat, greens and haricot beans plus fresh salad and as much bread as you want. *LD OPEN to 22.30 Mon-Sat. CLOSED Sun.* A. Ax. B. Dc.

Modhitis   **3 A 25**
83 Bayham St NW1. 01-485 7890. Greek Cypriot restaurant; mainly kebabs and casseroles. *LD OPEN to 23.30. CLOSED Sun.*

My Old Dutch   **3 I 26**
132 High Holborn WC1. 01-404 5008. Informal with student waiters and waitresses and an abundance of plants and rock music. 101 Dutch pancakes; some savoury, some dessert. *LD OPEN to 24.00 daily.* A. Ax. B. Cb. Dc.

Parsons   **4 L 4**
311 Fulham Rd SW10. 01-352 0651. Trendy and crowded Edwardian-style spaghetti house; potted palms and bentwood chairs. Hamburgers. Spaghetti and Mexican food, garlic bread and wine. Special meals for children. *LD OPEN to 00.30.* A. B. Dc.

Pizza Express   **3 H 24**
30 Coptic St WC1. 01-636 3232. Modern pizza parlour with a large red pizza oven in the middle. Many varieties. Good ice creams. Wine by the glass. Many branches. *LD OPEN to 24.00.*

Seashell   **2 A 17**
35 Lisson Gro NW1. 01-723 8703. Excellent fish and chip shop, take-away and sit down restaurant. *LD OPEN to 22.30. CLOSED Sun & Mon.*

Spaghetti House   **2 F 22**
15-17 Goodge St W1. 01-636 6582. Very busy, friendly restaurant. Separate kitchens on all three floors. Reasonably priced. Very good pastas and spaghettis. Cervella di vitello Milanese, saltimbocca alla Romana. Many branches. *LD OPEN to 23.00. (Sun 22.30).*

Standard Indian Restaurant
23 Westbourne Gro W2. 01-727 4818. Large, popular restaurant serving good Indian food at reasonable prices; a menu of over 80 specialities. Chicken tikka, butter chicken. *LD Reserve Sat & Sun. OPEN to 24.00.* A. Ax. B. Dc.

Stockpot   **5 J 21**
40 Panton St SW1. 01-839 5142. Crowded, noisy and excellent value. Home-made soups, casseroles and puds at popular prices. *LD OPEN to 23.30 Mon-Sat; to 22.00 Sun.* Also at 6 Basil St SW3.

Tuttons   **6 J 23**
11-12 Russell St WC2. 01-836 1167. Prices vary but you can eat here fairly cheaply and get good French food; best value is the plat du jour. *BLD OPEN to 00.30; Sun to 23.30.* A. Ax. B. Dc.

Outdoor eating

The Continental habit of eating outside can be very pleasant on a hot summer's day. The following places have a few tables on the pavement or in the garden. The Covent Garden Market area has many good outdoor eating restaurants, but also try South Molton St and Charlotte St.

Anemos   2 F 22

34 Charlotte St W1. 01-580 5907. Friendly, crowded and noisy, with customers and waiters singing and dancing on the tables. Eat outside at the pavement tables in summer. Humous, excellent kebabs, moussaka. *LD OPEN to 24.00. CLOSED Sun.* Children. **£.**

Au Bon Accueil   4 K 10

27 Elystan St SW3. 01-589 3718. Tables set out on the pavement in summer. Comfortable French restaurant with excellent cuisine. Escalope au rhum et orange, filet mignon sauce béarnaise. *LD Reserve. OPEN to 23.30. CLOSED Sun & L Sat.* A. Ax. Dc. **£.**

Froops

17 Princess Rd NW1. 01-722 9663. Bistro restaurant with a proper garden, partially covered and very full in summer. French provincial and Swedish dishes. *D Reserve. OPEN to 23.30. CLOSED Sun.* A. Ax. B. Dc. **££.**

The Rose Garden   2 A 20

Queen Mary's Rose Garden, Regent's Park NW1. 01-935 5729. Open-air eating in a London park at tables with parasols. Unadventurous English food but marvellous surroundings. *LD OPEN to 20.00.* **£.**

San Lorenzo Fuoriporta

38 Worple Rd Mews, Wimbledon SW19. 01-946 8463. Cheerful, lively trattoria with tables in the garden during summer. Ideal for Sunday lunches with children. Scalloppine di vitello alla San Lorenzo, petti di pollo, good fresh vegetables. *LD Reserve. OPEN to 23.00 Mon-Sat; to 22.00 Sun.* A. Ax. B. Dc. **££.**

Unusual eating

Beachcomber (Polynesian)   2 I 18

May Fair Hotel, Berkeley St W1. 01-629 7777. Hawaii and the South Seas, complete with alligators and tropical atmosphere. Polynesian food. Polynesian platter, chicken momi, tournedos Samoa. Happy hour *17.30-19.15* when drinks are served half price. *D Reserve. OPEN to 23.30. Dancing 20.45-01.30. CLOSED Sun.* A. Ax. B. Cb. Dc. **£££.**

My Fair Lady (Dinner Afloat)

Bookings and boarding from 250 Camden High St NW1. 01-485 4433/6210. Dine while you pass through the most picturesque stretch of the Regent's Canal. *Lunch cruise Sun only, board 12.30, sail at 13.00, cruise takes approx 2½ hrs. Dinner cruise Tue-Sat boarding at 19.30, sailing at 20.00, cruise takes approx 3 hrs* with popular entertainment. Also available for private hire. **£££.**

Flanagan's (Victorian fantasy)

11 Kensington High St W8. 01-937 2519.   **1 D   4**
Completely phoney (but enjoyable) Victorian 'dining rooms', with sawdust for spitting on, stalls, cockney songs and colourful signs, notices and extravaganza. Elegantly costumed waiters and serving girls (usually pleasantly independent Aussies). Tripe, jellied eels, game pie, enormous plates of fish and chips, golden syrup pudding. *LD OPEN to 23.15.* A. Ax. B. Cb. Dc. **£.**

Gallipoli (Belly dancers)   **6 N 32**
8 Bishopsgate Churchyard EC2. 01-588 1922. Exotic and unusual. Twice nightly cabaret of enjoyable and erotic Eastern belly dancing. Excellent Turkish food. Shish kebab, buryan Gallipoli, red mullet. *LD Reserve. OPEN to 02.00. CLOSED Sun. Cabaret 22.30 & 01.00.* A. Ax. B. Cb. Dc. **£££.**

Hispaniola (Dinner afloat)   **6 L 23**
The Thames at Victoria Embankment, Charing Cross WC2. 01-839 3011. A restaurant floating on the Thames. Romantic setting. Good Spanish food on upper or lower deck. *LD Reserve. OPEN to 23.20 (Sun 21.50).* B. Cb. Dc. **£££.**

Trader Vic's (South Seas)   **2 I 16**
London Hilton, Park La W1. 01-493 8000. Atmosphere of the Pacific islands and Orient in décor and food. South sea drinks. Tahitian fish soup, duckling barbecued, quenelles de Mahi Mahi. *LD OPEN to 23.45. CLOSED L Sat.* A. Ax. B. Cb. Dc. **££.**

Tudor Rooms (Medieval banquets)   **5 J 22**
80 St Martin's La WC2. 01-240 3978. Jesters and troubadours entertain while you eat your 5-course meal. Specialities include 'old' English beef, roast pork and chicken. *LD Reserve. OPEN to 02.00.* A. Ax. B. Cb. Dc. **£££.**

Villa dei Cesari
(Decadent Roman Empire)   **5 Q 15**
135 Grosvenor Rd SW1. 01-828 7453. Converted warehouse with good river views and terrace, decorated like a Roman villa. Band and dancing. Menu in Latin. *D Reserve. OPEN to 02.30. CLOSED Mon.* Ax. B. Dc. **£££.**

London's famous pubs

Most London pubs date back to the 19th C but many are up to 400 years old. Some take on the character and needs of the locality and are aptly called 'locals' while others provide cheerful places to relax for workers, shoppers or theatre-goers. The sheer number means that there will always be one close at hand no matter where in Central London you may be. Of the 7,000 pubs in London we have selected some of the most interesting, but there are many more to be discovered by the thirsty or the curious. Convivial and informal, these days pubs are no longer all-male preserves and provide a chance to meet new people.

Opening hours vary but usually 11.00-15.00 and 17.30-23.00 with early closing on Sun.

L-lunch; D-dinner; B-buffet. Most pubs serve snacks, some have hot buffet lunches and many have restaurants. These are indicated in the following list.

Bitter
The most popular beer which comes in two grades; ordinary and best. On draught or from the keg, the latter is the most expensive. All English beers are served at cellar temperature and are best savoured that way.

Mild
The least strong as its name implies.

Mixed
Half a pint of bitter mixed with half a pint of mild.

Stout
A very dark bottled beer. Guinness is the most popular variety and can be obtained on draught.

Barley wine
A very potent bottled drink equivalent in effect to a double whisky and much cheaper.

Lager
The nearest equivalent to the Continental beers. Usually served chilled on draught or bottled.

Cider
Rough cider on draught is hard to come by; bottled cider is sweeter.

Shandy
Can be bought made with equal amounts of bitter and lemonade, or bottled.

Light or Pale Ale
Bottled beer.

Brown Ale
Sweet dark bottled beer.

Ginger beer
Non-alcoholic fizzy drink, often used in shandy.

Baker and Oven 2 C 19

10 Paddington St W1. 01-935 5072. Small colourful orange and green pub with cosy basement alcoves and bars. Mouth watering home-made pies from 100-year-old baker's ovens. **B D**

Blackfriar 6 M 28

174 Queen Victoria St EC4. 01-236 5650. Triangular building in the shadows of Blackfriars railway bridge. Stunning shades of Art Nouveau mixed with Gothic; excellent buffet if you can get your eyes off the décor. **B**

Bunch of Grapes 1 I 11

207 Brompton Rd SW3. 01-589 4944. Popular Victorian pub with finely engraved 'snob-screens' separating the bars and impressively carved wooden pillars. **B**

Cheshire Cheese, Ye Olde 6 K 26

145 Fleet St EC4. 01-353 6170. Rebuilt after the Great Fire with low ceiling'd interiors, oak tables, sawdust on the floor. The pub probably hasn't changed much since Dr Johnson used to drop in. No snacks but good traditional English cooking for those in search of a meal. **L D**

Flask

77 Highgate West Hill N6. 01-340 3969. Famous, historic Highgate tavern where Dick Turpin once hid in the cellars and William Hogarth drew in the bar. English restaurant. **B L**

George Inn 6 Q 27

77 Borough High St SE1. 01-407 2056. Galleried Dickensian coaching inn mentioned in *Little Dorrit*. Excellent beer, dispensed from an unusual 'beer engine'. Wine bar with good selection of wines, pâtés and cheese. **L D**

Hole in the Wall 6 N 23

5 Mepham St SE1. 01-928 6196. Free house. Ednam's, Burke's, Brakspear, Ruddle and Young's cask bitters. Built in the arches by Waterloo Station with bar-loads of beer fanatics. **L D B**

Lamb and Flag 6 J 23

33 Rose St WC2. 01-836 4106. Originally called 'The Bucket of Blood' because the pub was the centre for fighting in the area (Dryden apparently got the 'once over' here). Now a popular mellow bar. **B**

London Apprentice

62 Church St, Old Isleworth, Middx. 01-560 1915. Thames-side 15th C pub with Elizabethan and Georgian interiors. Prints of Hogarth's 'Apprentices'. **L D B**

Museum Tavern 3 H 23

49 Gt Russell St WC1. 01-242 8987. Conveniently

located opposite the British Museum, the tavern attracts students and sightseers. Victorian interior with a mahogany bar and an abundance of engraved glass. **L B**

Nag's Head
79-81 Heath St NW3. 01-435 4108. Crowded every night with dedicated beer swillers sampling the impressive selection offered. Small patio. **B**

Orange   **5 M 12**
37 Pimlico Rd SW1. 01-730 5378. Nell Gwynn once sold oranges here. Cheerful atmosphere. **B**

Printer's Devil   **6 K 26**
98 Fetter La EC4. 01-242 2239. A printers' and journalists' pub named after the traditional printers' apprentice. Notable collection of early printing curios. **L B**

Prospect of Whitby
57 Wapping Wall E1. 01-481 1317. Tudor tavern overlooking the Thames. Samuel Pepys, Judge Jeffries, smugglers and thieves once drank here. Live music and French restaurant with balcony. **B L D**

St James's Tavern   **2 I 21**
45 Gt Windmill St W1. 01-437 5009. Large circular bar with gas lights, sawdusted floor and tiled mural scenes of Shakespeare's plays. English breakfast and afternoon tea as well as usual pub grub and drinks. **B L D**

Sherlock Holmes   **5 K 22**
10 Northumberland St WC2. 01-930 2644. Perfect replica of Holmes' study at 221b Baker St. **L D B**

Musical pubs
Jazz
Bricklayer's Arms
67 Ealing Rd, Brentford, Middx. 01-560 7841. Trad jazz and good bars. *Tue & Sat 20.30. Free.*

Bull's Head
373 Lonsdale Rd SW13. 01-876 5241. Home-cooked food. Modern jazz by top English and visiting foreign players *every night 20.00 & Sun lunch.*

Half Moon
93 Lower Richmond Rd SW15. 01-788 2387. Large pub with jazz *Sun L & eve, Tue & Wed eve.*

New Merlin's Cave   **3 G 29**
Margery St WC1. 01-837 2097. Barn-like pub offering *Sun lunchtime* jazz sessions. Top musicians drop in and play gratis.

Olde Gatehouse, Ye
Highgate West Hill N6. 01-340 2154. Reputed to be the oldest pub in Highgate. Jazz *Sun eve.*

Torrington
4 Lodge La N12. 01-445 4710. Well-known on the pub circuit for some top names in jazz rock. Visiting bands play in the restaurant. Jazz rock *Sun.* **B L**

Yorkshire Grey   **3 H 25**
2 Theobald's Rd WC1. 01-405 2519. Old fashioned, wood-panelled saloon with visiting musicians. Trad jazz *Fri & Sun.* **B**

Music hall – piano and singing
Queen's Head
83 Fieldgate St E1. 01-247 5593. Free and easy East End pub. Seamen and vodka. Old time piano music.

Pindar of Wakefield   **3 G 27**
328 Gray's Inn Rd WC1. 01-837 7269 (booking office 01-722 5395). The pub to go to for oldtime music-hall. *Thur, Fri & Sat nights* – book first for an excellent show. **L D B**

Rock
Golden Lion   **4 L 4**
490 Fulham Rd SW6. 01-385 3942. Good home-cooked lunches. Rock, blues, R&B. Rock *every eve.*

Greyhound
175 Fulham Palace Rd W6. 01-385 0526. *Every night.* Excellent value with no entrance fee. **B**

Hope and Anchor   **3 E 32**
207 Upper St N1. 01-359 4510. Beery pub with loud juke box upstairs, live music in the cellar *Mon-Sun* nights *from 21.00.* Open fires in winter.

Pied Bull   **3 D 32**
1 Liverpool Rd N1. 01-837 3218. Once Sir Walter Raleigh's house, now a pleasant pub. One bar has a stage. Rock *Mon, Tue, Thur, Fri & Sun.*

The Spurs
The Roundway N17. 01-808 4773. Thirties pub called after the football team, Tottenham Hotspur. Progressive heavy rock. Rock *Thur-Sun.* **B**

Drag pubs
Female impersonators enjoy an enormous popularity in pubs with acts that are a combination of blue jokes and songs. There is usually a roster of artistes who do the round of these better known pubs.

New Black Cap
171 Camden High St NW1. 01-485 1742. Two bars, one with photos of famous drag acts. *Every night & Sun L. Charge Thur-Sun.*

Royal Vauxhall Tavern
372 Kennington La SE11. 01-582 0833. *Every night & Sun L.*

Open air pubs
Anchor   6 O 28
Bankside SE1. 01-407 1577. 18th C replacement of original destroyed by fire of 1670. Five beamed bars and three restaurants — one with a minstrel's gallery. **L D B**

Black Lion
2 South Bank, Lion La W6. 01-748 7056. Lovely old riverside pub with a garden and grapevine. **L D B**

City Barge
27 Strand on the Green, Chiswick W4. 01-994 2148. 15th C riverside Elizabethan charter inn. **L B**

The Crown   5 O 21
35 Albert Embankment SW1. 01-735 1054. Lovely view over the river to the Houses of Parliament. **L B**

Dickens Inn   6 R 32
St Katharine's Way E1. 01-488 2208. Pub in the Dickensian style. Sit outside overlooking .the pleasure craft in St Katharine's Dock. **L D B**

Dove
19 Upper Mall W6. 01-748 5405. 16th C pub with verandah and good Thames view. **L D B**

Grapes
76 Narrow St E14. 01-987 4396. Traditional pub amid wharves and warehouses with balcony overlooking river. **B.**

Spaniards Inn
Hampstead La NW3. 01-455 3276. Famous 16th C inn with Dick Turpin and literary associations. Beer garden. **L B**

Theatre pubs
King's Head   3 E 32
115 Upper St N1. 01-226 1916. Probably the best known and most widely reviewed of theatre pubs. Decorated with theatre bills. You can have a meal before you see the show and stay at your table for the performance. *Lunchtime & evening* shows. Membership. **L D B**

Nag's Head   6 J 23
10 James St WC2. 01-836 4678. *Lunchtime* performances *Fri-Sat.* Lively Covent Garden pub decorated with theatrical playbills and prints. Good wine list. **D B**

The Orange Tree
45 Kew Rd, Richmond, Surrey. Bookings 01-940 3633. Popular performances by the excellent Orange Tree Theatre Group above this friendly, attractive pub. Take your drinks upstairs to watch the plays at *lunchtimes May-Aug* and in the *evenings Sept-Apr.* Small and informal. **D**

SHOPPING

London is one of the world's finest shopping centres, with a wonderful balance of luxury and utility shops; huge department stores and intimate boutiques; market stalls selling anything and everything and expensive specialist shops.

Shopping hours

Most shops in central London open at 09.30 hrs on weekdays, and stay open until 17.30 hrs. A few close early on Sat (13.00) but have one late-night opening during the week, usually on Thursday till 19.00 hrs. Shops in the suburbs stay open all day Sat, but have one early closing day in the week, nearly all the shops in that district will be closed for that afternoon.

Tourist Concessions

Most of the large department stores have Export Bureaux where overseas visitors can arrange to have their purchases sent abroad, free of Value Added Tax. EEC visitors, however, who exceed their allowances may be subject to customs duty on their return home, but the stores are familiar with the regulations of all countries and will advise you. They will also arrange the best delivery method for your purchases.

Souvenirs

All goods manufactured in England are the best buys. Dress and furnishing fabrics, particularly tweeds, cashmeres and woollens are of excellent quality and well worth the money. The ready-to-wear clothes in London rival those produced anywhere in the world in quality and design, so anything you buy in this line is likely to be fairly priced. Other worthwhile purchases are leather goods — coats, shoes and accessories; china, particularly Wedgwood, and porcelain; silver and antiques, rare books and prints. There are many shops geared for the tourist, with plastic Beefeaters etc. and almost everything has a Union Jack on it!

Markets

Markets are a colourful and vital part of London's trade and everyday life. These are the best known, aalthough there are literally hundreds of smaller street markets in the suburbs. They are still tremendously popular, and offer every kind of article from antiques and junk to food and household goods.

Berwick Street   2 H 21
Soho W1. General market in the heart of Soho: the fruit and vegetables are good, and prices reasonable, particularly at the southern end of the street. *OPEN 08.00-19.00 Mon-Sat.*

Camden Lock
Where Chalk Farm Rd crosses Regent's Canal NW6. Small antique, junk and bric-a-brac market. Also art and craft shops set in a cobbled courtyard beside the pretty lock and canal walks. Good hot food stand by the entrance. *OPEN 08.00-18.00 Sat & Sun.*

Camden Passage   3 E 32
Islington High St N1. A paved walk lined with a mixture of shops and stalls; the haunt of the trendies, selling a mixture of antiques and attractive, but expensive, bric-a-brac, particularly fine art-deco shop and opposite, a print shop which repays frequent visiting. *OPEN 09.00-18.00 Mon-Sat. Market days stalls OPEN 07.00-14.00 Tue, Wed & Sat.*

Leadenhall Market   6 O 31
Gracechurch St EC3. General retail market: vegetables, poultry, plants, fish and endless other items. The late Victorian glass and ironwork of the building is superb. *OPEN 09.00-17.00 Mon-Fri.* Shellfish on *Sun.*

Petticoat Lane   6 N 33
Radiates from Middlesex St E1. Huge bustling complex selling everything under the sun; some bargains, lots of rubbish but, most important, an atmosphere of fun. Some of the streets leading off the main road of stalls specialise in one type of thing e.g. **Club Row** deals in fish, birds, reptiles and mammals while neighbouring **Brick Lane** is good for furniture and electrical equipment. *OPEN Sun mornings only.*

Portobello Road   1 A 8
Nr Notting Hill Gate W11. Superb flea-market though now too well known for many bargains to exist. Vegetables, fruit and flowers. *OPEN 07.00-18.00 Mon-Sat* plus antiques, bizarre clothes and a welter of glorious junk. *OPEN Sat only.*

Conversion charts

Clothing Sizes

In London you will find both English, Continental and American sizing in the shops, whereas there is a combination of English and Continental sizing in the shoe shops.

Dresses

English	10	12	14	16	18	20	22
	32	**34**	**36**	**38**	**40**	**42**	**44**
USA		8	10	12	14	16	18	20
Continental	38	40	42	44	46	48	50

Shoes

English	3	$3\frac{1}{2}$	4	$4\frac{1}{2}$	5	$5\frac{1}{2}$	6	$6\frac{1}{2}$	7	$7\frac{1}{2}$	8
USA	$4\frac{1}{2}$	5	$5\frac{1}{2}$	6	$6\frac{1}{2}$	7	$7\frac{1}{2}$	8	$8\frac{1}{2}$	9	$9\frac{1}{2}$
Continental	35	36	37	37	38	38	39	40	40	41	41

Hats

English	$6\frac{5}{8}$	$6\frac{3}{4}$	$6\frac{7}{8}$	7	$7\frac{1}{8}$	$7\frac{1}{4}$	$7\frac{3}{8}$	$7\frac{1}{2}$	$7\frac{5}{8}$
USA	$6\frac{3}{4}$	$6\frac{7}{8}$	7	$7\frac{1}{8}$	$7\frac{1}{4}$	$7\frac{1}{2}$			
Continental	54	55	56	57	58	59	60	61	62

Glove sizes are international.

Weights and Measures

Feet/Metres

English	1	2	3	4	5	6	7	8	9	10
Continental	0.3	0.6	0.9	1.2	1.5	1.8	2.1	2.4	2.7	3.0

Pounds/Kilograms

English	1	2	3	4	5	6	7	8	9	10
Continental	0.4	0.9	1.4	1.8	2.3	2.7	3.2	3.6	4.1	4.5

Pints/Litres

English	$\frac{1}{4}$	$\frac{1}{2}$	$\frac{3}{4}$	1	2	3	4	5
Continental	0.1	0.3	0.4	0.6	1.1	1.7	2.3	2.8

Oxford street

     Charing Cross road

Left side	No.	No.	Right side
Fashion M **Homes**	4	5	Barclays Bank
Pub The **Tottenham**	6	7	**Coles** Fashion M
Restaurant **McDonalds**	8	⊖	Tottenham Court Road
		15	**K Shoes**
Employment agency **Reed**	12	17	Alfred Marks Employment Agency
Records **Virgin Records**	16	19	Regent School of Languages
Classic Cinema			Challoner Employment Agency
Jewellers **Herbert Wolf**	18	19	& school of English
Games Centre	22	19	Studio 21 Disco club
Fashion F **The Sale**	26	19	**Claude Gill** Books
Employment Agency **Rand**	34	25	**Crazy Sale** Fashion MF
Shoes **Barratts**	36	29	**Laganda** Restaurant
Jewellers **Michael Davis**	38	33	**Anello & Davide** Shoes
National Westminster Bank	40	37	**Electronics Superstore**
Bag Shop	40	37	Spats Club
Fashion **Mimika**	46	41	**Mates** Fashion F
Fast food **Hungry Fisherman**	46-48	43	**Cerex** Fashion M
		45	**John Kent** Fashion M
		47	**Guvnors** Fashion M
		49	Hearts of Oak & Enfield Building Society
Hanaway street		51	**The Leather Wagon** Boots
		51	**Arena Tours** Travel agent
Fashion **What she wants**	50	53	**Suede Leather & Sheepskin Shop**
Midland Bank	52	53	Rand Employment agency
		55	**Bricks** Fashion M
Rathbone place			**Soho street**
Tailors & hatters **Dunn & Co**	54	61	**Ratners** Jewellers
Fashion F **Santa's Exclusive**	58	61	Keystone Employment agency
Bank of Credit & Commerce International	62	63	Brook Street Employment agency
Employment agency **Atlas**	64	65	**London Leisure Centre** Arcade
Fashion F **Downtown**	66	67	**Tabcane** Shoes
Handbags **Salisburys**	68a	71	Churchill Employment agency
		71	City Centre Employment agency
		73	Hilton Cameras
Perry's place		73	Julia Bennett Photographic studios
		73	**Fashion for all** Fashion MF
Hi-fi **Sony JVC**	70	83	**Ablene** Oriental fashion F
Fashion F **Aristos**	72	85	**Marmalade** Fashion F
		87	**Wendy's** Hamburgers
Radio & hi-fi **Macdonald Stores**	78	89	**Greenfields** Fashion FM & camping centre
Books **Susan Reynolds**	80		
Shoes **Dolcis**	82		**Dean street**
Dixons Cameras	86	91	**The Rack** Fashion M
		93	**Card Shop** Posters & cards
		95	**Master Foto** Photo developer
		97	**Woodhouse** Fashion M
		101	**NW Souvenirs**
Newman street			**Great Chapel street**
Fashion M F **Irvine Sellers Mates**	90-92	103	**Masterland** Fashion market & souvenirs
Sight & Sound Secretarial Centre		103	**Leather Wagon Co** Shoes
Chemist **Underwoods**	94	105	Alfred Marks Employment agency
Video Film Mart	102	107	**The Shopping Centre**
100 Club	100		
Shoes **Manfield**	104		
Fashion M **Smith**	110		
National Westminster Bank	112		
Berners street			**Wardour street**
		127a	**Bewlays Pipes** Tobacconist
STORE **BOURNES STORE**		127	**Mister Byrite** Fashion M
		129	**Lord John** Fashion M
		133	**Athena Reproductions** Posters & prints
		137	**Harvest** Fashion F
		139	**Santas Fashion** Fashion F
		139	Grosvenor Nursing Service
		139	Church Bros Estate agents
Wells street			**Berwick street**
Supersports	134	145	**Taxi Driver** Fashion
Fashion M **Nickleby's**	136	147	**Fellini** Fashion
Souvenirs **Goldrange & Sons**	138	147	Josephine Sammons Employment agency
Fashion M **Take Six**	140	149	**Coles** Fashion M
		151	**Boots** Chemist
Restaurant **Wimpy**		153	**Jane Norman** Fashion F
Shoes **Dolcis**	146	155	**Greenfields** Fashion FM & camping centre
Employment agency **Acme**	146	159	**Shelley's** Shoes
Shopping precinct **Oxford Walk**			
Fashion M **Mr Kent**	156		**Poland street**
Shoes **Carvella**	158	161	**Ernest Jones** Jewellers
Fashion M **Mr Howard**	160	165	Academy Cinemas
Fashion F **Mates**	162	173	**MARKS & SPENCER** STORE
		175	**Freeman Hardy & Willis** Shoes
Winsley street		181	Kelly Girl Employment agency
		181	**Saxone** Shoes
Fashion F **Dorothy Perkins**	172	185	St Paul's Employment agency
Baby store **Mothercare**	174	185	Berni's Steak Bar Restaurant
Shoes **Peter Lord**	178	187	**The Paige shop** Fashion F

Oxford street continued

		187	Penberthy's *Fashion F*	

Great Titchfield street

Ramilles place

Shoes **Ravel**	184		199	**Zales** *Jewellers*
Fashion F **Marmalade**	190		201	**Our Price Records** *Records*
Shoes **Mr Henry**	192		213	**LITTLEWOODS** *STORE*
Restaurant **Quality Inn**	192		217	**Wallis** *Fashion F*
Midland Bank	196		219	**Ratners** *Jewellers*
STORE **C & A**	202			

Great Portland street

Hills place

Restaurant Café Torino	214		221	**John Walton** *Fashion M*
Fashion M **Peter Brown**	220		225	Studio Cinemas
Shoes **R P Ellen**	222		225	**Sacha** *Shoes F*
			231	**Jean Junction**
STORE **PETER ROBINSON**			231	**Lady Lisa** *Fashion F*
Fashion F **Top Shop**			231	Lighter Repair Centre
			233	**Mr Byrite** *Fashion F*
			235	Bank of Credit & Commerce

Argyll street

			241	**Finlays** *Tobacconist*
				Wedgwood Shop *China*
				Goldsmiths & Silversmiths *Shop*

Oxford circus

Regent street

				South African Airways
Fashion M **John Collier**	240		257	**Benetton** *Fashion FM*
Fashion F **Harper's House**	240		259	**Merceria** *Fashion F*
Fashion **Mister Byrite**	241		261	**Two-Six-One** *Leather and suede*
			263	**Richard Shops** *Fashion F*
John Prince's street			267	**Dorothy Perkins** *Fashion F*
			271	**Green & Symons** *Jewellery*
Travel agency Pontins	242		273	**Scottish Woollens**
Shoes **Bally**	246		275	Rink Club
Shoes **Ravel**	248		275	Salvation Army Hall
Jewellers **H Samuel**	250		277	**Ernest Jones** *Jewellers*
STORE **BRITISH HOME STORES**			283	**Girl** *Fashion F*
Shoes **Peter Lord**	252		285	**Jean Jeanie** *Fashion MF*
Fashion F **Jane Norman**	262		287	**Bata** *Shoes*
Shoes **Saddlers**	264		289	**Le Café Americain**
Jewellery **Zales**	266		291	**Brook Street** *Employment agency*
Fashion **Lord John**	268		291a	**Snob** *Fashion F*
Jeans **Bottom Line**	268		291b	National Westminster Bank
Fashion F **Wallis**	272			

Holles street

Harewood place

			293	**Saxone** *Shoes*
			299	**Babers** *Shoes*
			299	City Centre *Employment agency*
			299	L & D Nurses *Agency*
			299	Paris Academy *Fashion School*
			301	**Olympus Sport** *Sports goods*
STORE **JOHN LEWIS**			303	**Dolcis** *Shoes*
			309	**Werff (Berketex Bride)** *Fashion F*
Old Cavendish street			311	**WOOLWORTHS** *STORE*
			313	**Ratners** *Jewellers*
STORE **D H EVANS**			315	Acme *Employment agency*
			315	**Mates** *Fashion FM*

Chapel place

Dering street

K Shoes	324		321	Berlitz School of Languages
Regent Furs	326		325	**Lord John** *Fashion FM*
Jean Machine	328		325	**Manfield** *Shoes*
Bank of Scotland	332			

Vere street

New Bond street

STORE **DEBENHAMS**			333	**Dolcis** *Shoes*
			335	**NW Souvenirs**
Shoes **Dolcis**	350		337	**Footlights** *Shoes*
			337	**Sacha** *Shoes F*
			343	Indian Tea Centre *Restaurant*

Woodstock street

			351	**Sacha** *Shoes F*
			353	**Dormeuil** *Fabrics M*
Marylebone lane			353	Brook Street *Employment agency*
			355	**Oxford Textiles**
NW Souvenirs	354		357	**Jeans for You**
Fashion FM **Mates**	356		357	**Saddlers** *Shoes*
National Westminster Bank	358			

Sedley place

			359	**Denise** *Fashion F*
			361	**John Kent** *Fashion M*
			361	Find and Place *Employment agency*
			363	**HMV Records**
			369	**Paris Croissant** *Take-away food*
			369a	Town Tickets & Tours
			⊖	Bond Street
			373	**Ratners** *Jewellers*

Stratford place

Davies street

Shoes **Lilley & Skinner**	360		385	**West One** *Shopping Centre*
Fashion M **Take Six**	364		385	**Boots** *Chemist*
Fashion M **Michael Barrie**	366		393	**Coles** *Fashion M*
Fashion M **Lord John**	368		395	**Everon** *Fashion F*
Fashion F **Richard Shops**	372			

James street

Gilbert street

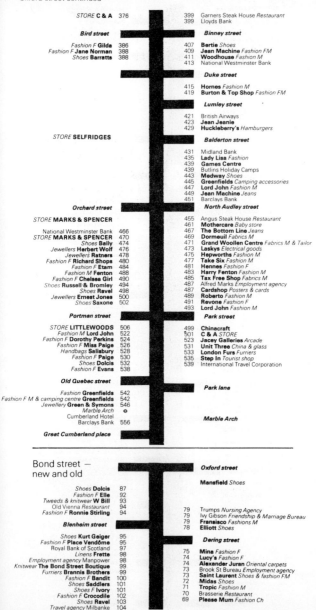

STORE **C & A**	376	399	Garners Steak House *Restaurant*
		399	Lloyds Bank

Bird street — **Binney street**

		407	**Bertie** *Shoes*
Fashion F **Gilda**	386	409	**Jean Machine** *Fashion FM*
Fashion F **Jane Norman**	388	411	**Woodhouse** *Fashion M*
Shoes **Barratts**	388	413	National Westminster Bank

Duke street

	415	**Hornes** *Fashion M*
	419	**Burton & Top Shop** *Fashion FM*

Lumley street

	421	British Airways
	423	**Jean Jeanie**
	429	**Huckleberry's** *Hamburgers*

STORE **SELFRIDGES**

Balderton street

	431	Midland Bank
	435	**Lady Lisa** *Fashion*
	439	**Games Centre**
	439	Butlins Holiday Camps
	443	**Medway** *Shoes*
	445	**Greenfields** *Camping accessories*
	447	**Lord John** *Fashion M*
	449	**Jean Machine** *Jeans*
	451	Barclays Bank

Orchard street — **North Audley street**

STORE **MARKS & SPENCER**		455	Angus Steak House *Restaurant*
		461	**Mothercare** *Baby store*
National Westminster Bank	466	467	**The Bottom Line** *Jeans*
STORE **MARKS & SPENCER**	470	469	**Dormeuil** *Fabrics M*
Shoes **Bally**	474	471	**Grand Woollen Centre** *Fabrics M & Tailor*
Jewellers **Herbert Wolf**	476	473	**Laskys** *Electrical goods*
Jewellers **Ratners**	478	475	**Hepworths** *Fashion M*
Fashion F **Richard Shops**	480	477	**Take Six** *Fashion M*
Fashion F **Etam**	484	481	**Hennes** *Fashion F*
Fashion F **Fenton**	488	483	**Harry Fenton** *Fashion M*
Fashion F **Chelsea Girl**	490	485	**Tax Free Shop** *Fabrics M*
Shoes **Russell & Bromley**	494	487	Alfred Marks *Employment agency*
Shoes **Ravel**	498	487	**Cardshop** *Posters & cards*
Jewellers **Ernest Jones**	500	489	**Roberto** *Fashion M*
Shoes **Saxone**	502	491	**Revone** *Fashion F*
		493	**Lord John** *Fashion M*

Portman street — **Park street**

STORE **LITTLEWOODS**	506	499	**Chinacraft**
Fashion M **Lord John**	522	501	**C & A** *STORE*
Fashion F **Dorothy Perkins**	524	523	**Jacey Galleries** *Arcade*
Fashion F **Miss Paige**	526	531	**Unit Three** *China & glass*
Handbags **Salisbury**	528	533	**London Furs** *Furriers*
Fashion F **Paige**	530	535	**Step In** *Tourist shop*
Shoes **Dolcis**	532	539	International Travel Corporation
Fashion F **Evans**	538		

Old Quebec street — **Park lane**

Fashion **Greenfields**	542	
Fashion F M & camping centre **Greenfields**	542	
Jewellery **Green & Symons**	546	
Marble Arch	⊖	**Marble Arch**
Cumberland Hotel		
Barclays Bank	556	

Great Cumberland place

**Bond street —
new and old**

Oxford street

Mansfield *Shoes*

Shoes **Dolcis**	87	79	Trumps *Nursing Agency*
Fashion F **Elle**	92	79	Ivy Gibson *Friendship & Marriage Bureau*
Tweeds & knitwear **W Bill**	93	79	**Fransisco** *Fashions M*
Old Vienna *Restaurant*	94	78	**Elliott** *Shoes*
Fashion F **Ronnie Stirling**	94		

Blenheim street — **Dering street**

Shoes **Kurt Geiger**	95	75	**Mina** *Fashion F*
Fashion F **Place Vendôme**	95	74	**Lucy's** *Fashion F*
Royal Bank of Scotland	97	74	**Alexander Juran** *Oriental carpets*
Linens **Frette**	98	73	Brook St Bureau *Employment agency*
Employment agency **Manpower**	98	73	**Saint Laurent** *Shoes & fashion FM*
Knitwear **The Bond Street Boutique**	99	72	**Midas** *Shoes*
Furriers **Brannia Brothers**	99	71	**Tropic** *Fashion M*
Fashion F **Bandit**	100	70	Brasserie *Restaurant*
Shoes **Saddlers**	101	69	**Please Mum** *Fashion Ch*
Shoes F **Ivory**	101		
Fashion F **Crocodile**	102		
Shoes **Ravel**	103		
Travel agency **Milbanke**	104		

Bond street continued

Fashion **Daniel Hechter**	105
Office stationers **Ryman**	106
Fashion F **Lucy's**	107
Fashion M **Chavila**	108
Employment agency St Paul's	108
Hairdresser **Stephen Way**	109
Raymond Young Private Clinic	109
Shoes **Russell & Bromley**	109
Barclays Bank	
Bond Street Gallery	111
Fashion F **Saint Laurent**	113
Shoes **Magli**	114
Employment agency Alfred Marks	115
Shoes **Bally**	116
Jewellers & silversmiths **Crombie**	118
Book Keepers Bureau	118
Employment agency Winfred Johnson	118
Employment agency Rand	119
Fashion M **Cecil Gee**	122
Oriental carpets **T. Zuber**	123
Arcade **Bond Street Antique Centre**	124
Marriage bureau **Heather Jenner**	124
Graus Antiques	125
Fashion M **Herbie Frogg**	125
Cameras **Wallace Heaton**	127
Midland Bank	129

Grosvenor street

Chinacraft	130
Fashion M **Beale & Inman**	131
Fashion F **Fiorucci**	133
Fashion F **Gorgissima**	134
Fashion M **Serge**	135
Paris Carpet Company	137
Fashion F **Marie Claire**	138
Silver & goldsmiths **S. J. Phillips**	139
Fashion M **Ascott**	140
Olympic Airways	141
Fashion M **Polo Ralph Lauren**	143
London Academy of Modelling	143
Antiques **Frank Partridge**	144
Fine art dealers **Wildenstein**	147
Fine Art Society	148
Luggage **Henry's**	149
Fashion & travel **Ireland House**	150

Bruton street

Luxury goods **Hermés**	152
Fashion F **Emanuel Ungaro**	153a
Jewellery **Bonds**	153
Air France	158
National Westminster Bank	159
Barclays Bank	161
Employment agency **Kelly Girl**	161
Shoes M **Churches**	163
Fashion F **Ted Lapidus**	163

Grafton street

Luxury accessories **Asprey**	165
Fashion Ch **Rowes**	
Leather goods **Nazareno Gabrielli**	171
Fashion F **Ports**	172
Fashion F **Chloé**	173
Fashion F **Robina**	174
Jewellers **Cartier**	175
Shoes & leatherwear **Rossetti**	177
Jewellers **Chaumet**	178
Jewellers **Kutchinsky**	179
Jewellers **Boucheron**	180
Silver & goldsmiths **Carringtons**	180
Leather goods **Loewe**	25
Luxury goods **Gucci**	27
The **Royal Arcade**	28
Silver & jewellery **Holmes**	29
Model agency Gavin L. B. **Robinson**	30
Shoes **Bally**	30
Beauty salon **Yardley**	33

Stafford street

Midland Bank	36
Leather goods **Andrew Soos**	37
Diamond merchants **Charig**	38
Marlborough Fine Art Gallery	39
Lloyds Bank	39
Employment **Success after 60**	40
Horizon Holidays	40-41

68	**Myers** Office equipment
68	**Carvella** Shoes
67	**Rivoli** Fashion F
66	**Rayne Shoes** Shoes
65	**Bently & Co** Jewellers
64	**Dixons** Cameras

Brook street

FENWICKS STORE

55	Bernadette Bureau Employment agency
54	**Smythson of Bond Street** Leather goods
53	**Jasons** Fabrics
51	**The White House** Linen
50	**Chapell Music Centre**
47	**Pinet** Shoes

Maddox street

46	**Khan Carpets**
45	**Campkins Camera Centre**
43	**Régine** Fashion F
42	**Stanley Lowe** Fabrics
41	**Frost & Reed** Paintings
40	**Mallett & Son** Antiques
38	**Herbie on Bond St** Fashion M
37	**Gerald Austin** Fashion M
36	**Maxwell** Shoes
34	Sotheby Auctioneer
31	**Bond Street Carpets**
30	**Hubert** Fashion M
29	**César** Fashion M
28	**Céline** Accessories F
27	**Yazdani Gallery** Paintings
26	**Tessiers** Gold & silversmiths
25	**Russell & Bromley** Shoes FM

Conduit street

23	**Philip Landau** Fashion M
23	**Cuero** Suede & leather
22	**Fior** Jewellery
22	**Rachel Child** Antiques
21	Indian Tourist Office
20	**Elizabeth Arden** Beauty salon
18	Aerolineas Argentinas
17	Air India

Clifford street

16	Watches of Switzerland
16	**Stephen Peters** Fashion M
15	**George Jensen** Silversmith
14a	**Piaget** Watches
13	**Oriental Carpet Galleries**
14	**Loja Brasileira** Carpets
12	**Janet Reger** Lingerie
11	**Philip Antrobus** Jewellers
10a	**Adèle Davis** Fashion F
10	**Anne Bloom** Jewellers
9a	**Booty** Jewellers
9	**The Platinum Shop** Jewellery
8	**Trouser House** Fashion M
8	**John Mitchell** Fine paintings
6	**Etienne Aigner** Fashion MF
5	**Rolex** Watches
4	**Richard Green** Art gallery
1	National Westminster Bank

Burlington gardens

24	**Feragamo** Shoes & accessories
23	**Truefitt & Hill** Hair salon M
23	**Rare Carpet Gallery**
22	**D Nata** Travel
19	**A Sulka & Company** Fashion M
17	**Wylma Wayne** Art
17	**Rashid Carpet**
17	**Clough** Antiques
16	**Courrèges** Fashion M
16	**Delman** Shoes
14	**Rayne House** Shoes
14	**Colnaghi Galleries** Paintings
13	**Leger Galleries** Paintings
13	**Benson & Hedges** Tobacconist
12	Ghana Airways
11	**Brainin Cashmeres**
10	**The Shaw College** Beauty
9	**Argos**
9	**Silver Crystal Suite** Crystal goods
7	**Mayfair Carpet gallery**
7	**Lloyd Jennings** Shoes M
6	The Embassy Club

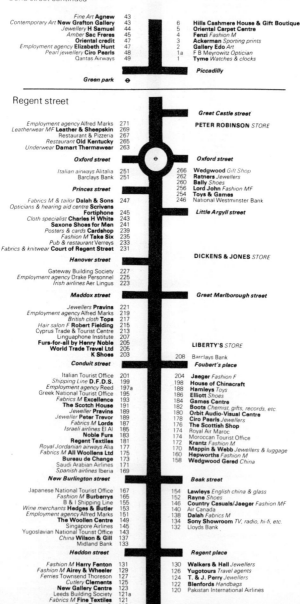

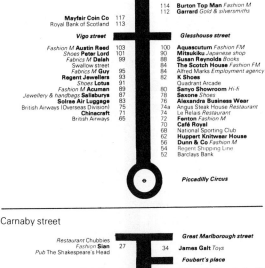

Left		Right	
Mayfair Coin Co	117	114	**Burton Top Man** *Fashion M*
Royal Bank of Scotland	113	112	**Garrard** *Gold & silversmiths*
Vigo street			*Glasshouse street*
Fashion M **Austin Reed**	103	100	**Aquascutum** *Fashion FM*
Shoes **Peter Lord**	101	90	**Mitsukiku** *Japanese shop*
Fabrics M **Dalan**	99	88	**Susan Reynolds** *Books*
Swallow street		84	**The Scotch House** *Fashion FM*
Fabrics M **Guy**	95	84	Alfred Marks *Employment agency*
Regent Jewellers	93	82	**K Shoes**
Shoes **Lotus**	91		Quadrant Arcade
Fashion M **Acuman**	89	80	**Sanyo Showroom** *Hi-fi*
Jewellery & handbags **Salisburys**	87	78	**Saxone** *Shoes*
Solrae Air Luggage	83	76	**Alexandra Business Wear**
British Airways (Overseas Division)	75	74a	**Angus Steak House** *Restaurant*
Chinacraft	71	74	Le Relais *Restaurant*
British Airways	65	72	**Fenton** *Fashion M*
		70	**Café Royal**
		68	**National Sporting Club**
		62	**Huppert Knitwear House**
		56	**Dunn & Co** *Fashion M*
		54	Regent Shipping Line
		52	Barclays Bank

Piccadilly Circus

Carnaby street

Left		Right	
			Great Marlborough street
Restaurant Chubbies			
Fashion **Sian**	27	34	**James Galt** *Toys*
Pub The Shakespeare's Head			*Foubert's place*
Fashion F **Lady Lisa**	33	31	**Supreme Fashions** *Fashion FM*
Souvenirs **Gear**	35	30	**Sir Harry** *Fashion M*
		29	**Lady Jane** *Fashion F*
Arcade **Carnaby Court**		28	**Raj Enterprises** *Indian fashions*
Merc Jeans Shop		28a	**Fancy That of London** *Souvenirs*
Fashion F M **Flea Market**			
Fashion F M **Anitas**	39		*Lowndes court*
Souvenirs **Cerex**	40	26	**Chandis** *Fashion FM*
Jean Masters	41	25	**Ruby Fashions** *Fashion FM*
Gifts & bags **Ladylord**	42		*Marlborough court*
Fashion F **Melanddi**	43	24	**Soccer Scene** *Sports shop*
		23	**Donis** *Fashion M*
		22	**Carnaby Fashion** *Fashion F*
		21	**Kay Boutique** *Fashion FM*
Fashion F **Ruby Fashions**	44		*Ganton street*
Fashion F **Topper**	44		
Pipes & tobacco **Inderwicks**	45	20	**Superama**
Gifts **The Personalised Gift Shop**	46a	15	**Snoopy Shop** *Gifts*
Fashion F **2nd Gear**	46	14	**Catch** *Fashion F*
Fashion F **Ruby Fashions**	47	13	**Daedalus** *Gifts*
Fashion & gifts **Kleptomania**	47a	12	**Rawhide** *Leather fashions*
Jewellery & gifts **Fairmart**	48	11	**Cerex** *Souvenirs*
Carnaby Sporting Club	49	10	**Melanddi** *Shoes*
Fashion Ch **Kids in Gear**	49	9	**Raj Enterprises** *Fashion FM*
Jewellery **The Great Frog**	50	8	**Depot** *Gifts & clothes*
Lisa Drugstore	52	6	**Cascade** *Arcade of shops*
Indian Fashions **Mina**	56	5	**Liza Super Store**
Leatherwear & glass **Anchorage Arts**	57	4	**Leatherfair**
		3	**Minar** *Gifts*
		2	**Mina** *Indian fashions*

Beak street

Kings road

Left		Right	
Sloane square			Sloane square
STORE **PETER JONES**		27	**Kamikazi** *Fashion F*
		27a	**Midas** *Shoes FM*
		9	Post Office
		11	**Broomfields** *Bakery*
			HoHo *Restaurant*
		13	**International Supermarket** *Food store*
		17	**NSS** *Newsagents & tobacconists*
		19	**Victoria Wine**
		21	Ladbrokes *Turf accountant*
		23	Brook Street *Employment agency*
		25	**Keep in Touch** *Fashion FM*
		25	**Club Masterview** *Employment agency*
Cadogan gardens		27	**Paris Link** *Fashion FM*
		29	**Boots** *Chemist*

Shoes **Lilley & Skinner**	34		Duke of York's Headquarters
London School of Bridge	34		
Our Price Records	36		
Fashion F Sidney Smith	35		
Fashion M **Cecil Gee**	44		
Restaurant & wine bar Blushes	46		
Hair salon **Sissors**	46a		
Shoes **Chelsea Cobbler**	54		
Fashion FM **Razzi**	54		
Restaurant Le Café Americain	56		
Chemist **Underwood**	58		
Shoes **Russell & Bromley**	64		
Shoes **Dolcis**	68		
Blacklands terrace			
Fashion FM **Lord John**	72		
Lincoln street			
			Cheltenham terrace
Restaurant Guys & Dolls	74		
Shoes **Saddler**	76	33	National Westminster Bank
Restaurant Pizzaland	80	33a	**Family** *Fashion FM*
Fashion F **Irvine Sellers**	82	33b	**Fiorucci** *Fashion F*
Shoes **Hobbs**	84	33c	Don Luigi *Restaurant*
Shoes **Sacha International**	86	33d	**Monsoon** *Fashion F*
Fashion F **Ronnie Stirling**	88	33e	**Martins** *Radios*
Fashion F **Girl**	90		Texaco *Petrol station*
Shoes **Bally**	92		
Fashion F **Benetton**	94		**Walpole street**
Fashion F **Wallis**	96		
Restaurant The Chelsea Kitchen	98	35	Safeways *Supermarket*
Wines Peter Dominic	100		
Fashion F **Wakefords**	102		
Anderson street			
Chelsea Building Society	112		
Fashion M **Reiss**	114		
Tryon street			**Royal avenue**
Fashion M **Just Men**	118		
Shoes **Bertie**	118		
Shoes **Elliot**	120		
Optician **Clulow**			
Shoes **Mr Henry**			
Supermarket Sainsbury			
Chemist **Boots**			
Fashion M **Oscars**	122a		
Fashion F **Kite**	124		
Shoes F **Katrina**	124		
Shoes **Kickers**	128	49	**Harlequin** *Arcade store*
Bureau de change Chequepoint	130	49	Chelsea Drugstore *Disco bar*
Beauty products **Yves Rochet**	132	51	Playboy Bookmakers *Turf accountant*
		55	**Andrews** *Butchers*
		57	**Slot Machine** *Fashion F*
		57	**Carré** *Fashion M*
Bywater street			**Wellington square**
Bakery **Beaton's**	134	61	**Gee 2** *Fashion M*
Fashion **Anita's**	136	63	**Robert Fielding** *Hair Salon & wigs*
Pub The **Markham**	138	65	**The Body Shop** *Natural cosmetics*
Markham Pharmacy	138a	67	**Take 6** *Fashion M*
		67a	**Strings** *Fashion M*
Markham square		69	**Take 6** *Fashion M*
Barclays Bank	140		**Smith street**
Shoes **Shelly's**	146		
		71	**Lord John Executive** *Fashion M*
Markham street		71	**Jones** *Fashion F*
		75	**Chopra** *Fashion FM*
Fashion F **Tomato**		80	**Koko** *Fashion F*
Hair & beauty FM **Neville Daniel**		80	**Review** *Fashion FM*
Restaurant The **Pheasantry**		83	**Downtown** *Fashion F*
		84	**Great Gear Market** *Fashion*
		85	**Reflections** *Restaurant*
		87a	**Serge** *Fashion M*
		89	**Second Image** *Fashion FM*
		91	Good Earth *Restaurant*
		93	**Le Bistingo** *Fashion F*
		97	**New Boxer** *Fashion M*
			Car Park
		101	**Hanky Panky** *Fashion Ch*
		103	**Carvil** *Fashion M*
		105	**105 King's Road** *Fashion F*
		107	Wedgies Club
		107	**The Campus Shop** *Fashion M*
		109	**Campus** *Fashion M*
		109	Christian Science *Reading Room*
Stationery **Ryman**		113	**Rivaaz** *Fashion F*
		115	**Jean Centre** *Fashion FM*
Jubilee place			
			Radnor walk
Lloyds Bank	164		
Chelsea Leather	168	119	Chelsea Potter *Pub & restaurant*
Stationery **Scribbler**	170		
Restaurant Choy's	172	121	**The Common Market** *Fashion FM*
Fashion F **Jake**	174		**The Department Store**
Fashion F **Miss Chelsea**	176	123	Victoria Wine
		125	**Pinto for Men** *Fashion M*
Burnsall street			

Left side			Right side	
Fashion M **Tipo**	178			
Shoes **R. Soles**	178a			
Fashion F **Pik Lik**	182a			

Shawfield street

125	**Pinto** Fashion FM
127	Dino's Restaurant
129	**Jones** Fashion M
135	**Antiquarius** Antiques, fashion, jewellery, etc.

Left		
Shoe repairs **We Heel**	184	
Electrical Equipment **Ashby**	184	
Fashion F **Ibiza**	184a	

137	**Antiquarius**
139	**Antiquarius** Antiques, fashion, jewellery, etc.
141	**Antiquarius**

Dry cleaners **Sketchley** 186a

Flood street

Fashion FM **Soldier Blue** 188
Fashion F **Sunny Side** 188a
Fashion M F **Blue Max** 188a
Restaurant American Hamburger **The Kings Rd** 190
Leathers 192
Handbags **Shura** 192
Waitrose
Pub **Trafalgar** 200

145	**Jaeger** Fashion FM
147	**Pepe at St Tropez** Fashion FM
151	**Omcar** Fashion MF
151	W. M. Jones Opticians
153	**Boy** Fashion M
155	**Ducati** Fashion MF
155a	CHELSEA METHODIST CHURCH
157	**Harvid Book Store**
159	**G Dutton** Shoes
161	**Jean Machine** Fashion FM

Furnishings **Habitat**

Chelsea Manor street

	TOWN HALL
181	**Chenil Galleries**
185	**Mens** Fashion FM
187	**Camera Craft**
191	**Flip** Fashion MF
193	**Ace** Fashion F
193	**Musique** Disco & restaurant
197	The Six Bells Pub
199	**Hide Park** Antiques & leather furniture
201	**Chelsea Wash Inn** Launderette
203	**Chelsea Record Centre**
205	**Pucci Pizza Vino** Restaurant
207	**Givans** Linen
209	**Superwines**

National Westminster Bank 224
Post Office 232
Household **Reject Shop**

Sydney street

COUNCIL OFFICES 250

Dovehouse street

CHELSEA FIRE STATION

Manresa road

COLLEGE OF SCIENCE & TECHNOLOGY

Oakley street

Glebe place

219	**Tiger Tiger** Toys
221	**The Bouzy Rouge** Wine shop & bar
229	**P. W. Forte** Fashion FM
231	**Rider Footwear**
237	**Chelsea Food Fayre**
239	**Bastet** Fashion F

Bramerton street

Fashion Ch **Small Wonder** 296

241	**Meeny's** Fashion
243	**The 243 Shop** Newsagent & tobacconist
245	**D. Kirkham** Greengrocer
245	**Antique Market**
247	**Joanna Booth** Antiques
249	Dominic's Restaurant
251	**S. Boris** Delicatessen
253	**Chelsea Antique Market**
255	**Jeremy** Antiques
257	**Green & Stone** Artists' materials
263	**Topaz** Accessories MF
	Chelsea Travel Agency
267	**Isaac Lloyd** Chemist
269	**David Pettifer** Antiques
271	**Designers Guild** Furnishings
271b	Borshtch 'n' Cheers Restaurant
275	**David Tron** Antiques
277	**Designers Guild** Fabric & wallpapers

Estate agency Jackson Rose 296a
Pub **Cadogan Arms** 298

Old Church street

	Classic Cinema
279	**Mr Light** Lighting
279	**Europa Foods**
281	**B&V** Gifts
283	**M. Silver & Sons** Jewellers
285	**Gilbert Parr** Sculptures
287	Raffles Club
289	**Sasha Hetherington** Fashion F
289	Kings Road Jam Restaurant
	Joanna's Tent Fashion F

National Westminster Bank 300
Interior designers Osborne & Little 304

Design Direction 308
Antiques **Richard Godson** 310
Restaurant Le Gourmet 312
Artists' materials **Chelsea Art Stores** 314
Restaurant Kennedy's 316
Antiques **David Tremayne** 320
Antiques **R. Weam & Son** 322
Picture framing Alfred Hecht 324
Carpets **Bernadout** 328
Restaurant Toscanini 330
Restaurant Le Bistingo 334
Kings Rd Cellars 336
Fashion **New Masters** 336
Restaurant Queenie's 338
Fabrics **Liberty Prints** 340a
Restaurant Thierry 342
Antiques **Tony Bunzl** 344
Barclays Bank 348

Paultons square

The Vale

GLC Ambulance station

303	**Hoopper & Purchase** Antique furniture
	Bamboo Kitchen Chinese take-away
305	**Chelsea Hi-fi**
307	**Ciancimino** Furniture antique & modern
311	**Fruit Fly** Fashion
309a	**Robot** Fashion MF

Stores Tel. nos.
Aquascutum 734 6090
Army & Navy 834 1234
Asprey 4936767
Austin Reed 734 6789
Barkers 937 5432
Building Centre 637 9001
C&A 629 7272
Cartier 493 6962
Christies 839 9060
Debenhams 580 3000
Design Centre 839 8000
Dickins & Jones 734 7070
D.H. Evans 629 8800
Fenwick 629 9161
Fortnum & Mason 734 8040
Foyles 437 5660
General Trading Company 730 0411
Habitat (Kings Rd) 351 1211
Habitat 388 1721
Hamleys 734 3161
Heals 636 1666
Harrods 730 1234
Harvey Nichols 235 5000
HMV 629 1240
Jaeger 734 8211
John Lewis 629 7711
Laura Ashley 730 1771
Liberty 734 1234
Lillywhites 930 3181
Maples 387 7000
Marks & Spencer (Marble Arch)
935 7954
Marks & Spencer (Oxford St) 734 4904
Marks & Spencer 507 4331
Mothercare 629 6621
Peter Jones 730 3434
Peter Robinson 636 7700
Selfridges 629 1234
Simpson 734 2002
Sotheby's 493 8080
The Market (Covent Garden) 836 9137
Virgin Megastore 631 1234

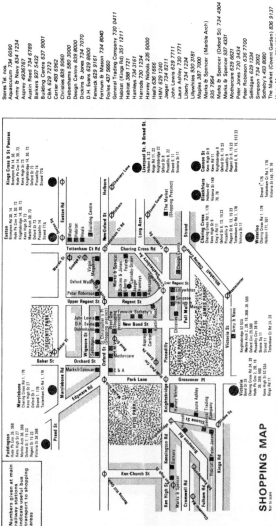

SHOPPING MAP
Not to scale

© Copyright Robert Nicholson Publications

GETTING ⊖UT

Airports

All the airports servicing London are quite a distance outside the city. If you wish to reach them by car you will find ample parking facilities for both brief and long periods. The easiest way of getting to Heathrow is by the special London Transport buses or by the Piccadilly line on the underground, and to Gatwick by train from Victoria Station. There is a regular coach service to Luton from Victoria coach station (see below). All airports are amply provided with shops, banks, and other necessary facilities for passengers.

London Gatwick Airport
Horley, Surrey. Crawley 28822.
London Heathrow Airport
Bath Rd, Heathrow, Middx. 01-759 4321.
Luton Airport
Luton, Beds. Luton 36061.

Air terminals

Check-in facilities for most major airlines are now based at the airports. For information or advice, contact airline booking offices. See telephone directories for details.
British Caledonian   **5 M 15**
Central London Air Terminal, Victoria Station SW1.
01-834 9411. *OPEN 24 hrs.*

Airport bus services

London Transport
A1 Heathrow, Cromwell Rd, Victoria. *Daily, every 20 minutes; 06.40-20.40, then at 21.10 and 21.40.*
A2 Heathrow, Bayswater, Paddington. *Daily, every half-hour 06.35-21.35.*
Flightline
757 Luton, Victoria, *every half-hour.*
767 Heathrow, Victoria, *every half-hour.*
777 Gatwick, Victoria, *every half-hour.*
Enquiries for both London Transport and Flightline services: 01-222 1234.

Rail terminals

British Rail Travel Centre   **5 J 20**
4-12 Lower Regent St SW1. Personal callers only.
Booking centre for rail travel in Britain and rail and
sea journeys to the Continent and Ireland. Several
languages spoken. See also under 'Information
centres'.

Charing Cross *(South)*
Strand WC2. Information 01-928 5100.

Euston *(North)*
Euston Rd NW1. Information 01-387 7070.

King's Cross *(North)*
Euston Rd N1. Information 01-278 2477.

Liverpool Street *(East & Continental)*
Liverpool St EC2. Information 01-283 7171.
Continental 01-834 2345.

Paddington *(West)*
Praed St W2. Information 01-262 6767.

Victoria *(South & Continent)*
Terminus Place, Victoria St SW1. Information
01-928 5100. Continental 01-834 2345.

Waterloo *(South)*
York Rd SE1. Information 01-928 5100.

Other rail services:
Motorail
Car bookings for the Continent 01-928 5151.
Sealink
Sealink Travel Centre, Victoria Station SW1. General
information and enquiries 01-834 2345.

Buses and underground

Green Line Buses
Enquiries: 01-222 1234.
Operate a regular service to approx 30 miles from
London. The main picking up points are at
Buckingham Palace Rd, Eccleston Bridge, Oxford
Circus and Regent St.

London Transport buses & underground
Enquiries: 01-222 1234.
Free maps of all London bus routes and the
underground system are available from underground station ticket offices.

Coach stations

Victoria Coach Station   **5 M 14**
164 Buckingham Palace Rd SW1. 01-730 0202. The

main provincial coach companies operate from here, travelling all over Britain and the Continent. Booking necessary.

Day trips from London

Cheap day excursion and special country afternoon tickets are available to most places by rail. Buses and coaches leave regularly from Victoria Coach Station.
EC = early closing day.

Blenheim Palace
Woodstock, Oxfordshire. Woodstock 811325. A great classical style ducal palace by Sir John Vanbrugh 1705-22. The estate was given by Queen Anne to John Churchill, Duke of Marlborough for his victory over Louis XIV at Blenheim in 1704. Winston Churchill was born here. Fine paintings, tapestries and furniture. The park was landscaped first by Wise and later by Capability Brown in 1760, who dammed the small stream to create two great lakes, keeping Vanbrugh's original bridge, and forming a dam ingeniously separating the two levels of water. London 60 miles (A34). *OPEN Mar-Oct 11.30-17.00 Mon-Sun. Charge.*

Brighton, E. Sussex
Known as 'Little London by the sea', this once poor fishing village has been a lively, bustling seaside resort ever since the Prince Regent set up his court in the fabulous Oriental-domed Pavilion. Fashionable shops, splendid Regency terraces, good pubs and restaurants, cockle stalls, fairs and sport of all kinds. 5 miles of beach and a magical Victorian pier. Train 1 hr. *EC Wed or Thur.* London 48 miles (A23).

Cambridge
A great university of spires, mellow colleges and riverside meadows, bordering the Cam. The famous 'Backs' and the lovely bridges are best seen by hiring a punt. The 20 or so colleges are from the

13th C onwards including Trinity by Wren, Kings by James Gibbs and the modern Queens by Basil Spence. The city contains the superb Fitzwilliam Museum, the notable Botanic Garden and some fine churches. Train 1½ hrs. *EC Thur.* London 55 miles (A10).

Canterbury, Kent
Pleasant old walled city on the river Stour, dominated by the magnificent Gothic cathedral, containing the shrine of Thomas à Becket (murdered 1170) and the tomb of the Black Prince. Good local museum in West Gate. Train 1½ hrs. *EC Thur.* London 56 miles (M2).

Chichester, W. Sussex
An old Roman city walled by the Saxons and graced by its beautiful 12th C cathedral. Now mostly Georgian in character. Fine 16th C Butter Cross, a medieval Guildhall and modern Festival Theatre, built 1962. Excellent harbour for sailing. Train 1½ hrs. *EC Thur.* London 63 miles (A3, A286).

Ham House
Petersham, Surrey. 01-940 1950. Superb 17th C country house built on an 'H' plan. Lavish Restoration interior. Important collection of Stuart furniture. *OPEN Apr-Oct 14.00-18.00 Tue-Sun & B. hols; Nov-Mar 12.00-16.00 Tue-Sun. Small charge.*

Hampton Court Palace
Hampton Court, Middx. 01-977 8441. Royal palace built 1514 for Cardinal Wolsey with later additions

by Henry VIII and Wren. Sumptuous state rooms painted by Vanbrugh, Verrio and Thornhill. Famous picture galley of Italian masterpieces. Orangery, mellow courtyards, the 'great vine' and the maze. The formal gardens are probably among the greatest in the world. Exotic plants from 16th C. (The Mitre opposite). *OPEN Apr-Sept 09.30-18.00 Mon-Sat, 11.00-18.00 Sun. Oct-Mar 09.30-17.00 Mon-Sat, 14.00-17.00 Sun. Charge.*

Hatfield
Hatfield, Herts. Hatfield 62823. A mellow and completely preserved Jacobean mansion with magnificent interior built in 1607-11 by Robert Cecil, 1st Earl of Salisbury and still the home of the Cecil

family. The Tudor Old Royal Palace nearby was the home of Queen Elizabeth I. Collection of 16th, 17th and 18th C portraits, manuscripts and relics. London 20 miles (A1). For Elizabethan banquets tel Hatfield 62055, all year. *House OPEN 25th Mar-10th Oct 12.00-17.00 Tue-Sat, 14.00-17.30 Sun. 11.00-17.00 B. hols. Charge.*

Marble Hill House

Richmond Rd, Twickenham, Middx. 01-892 5115. Palladian-style house built in 1728 by Roger Morris, with interior and furnishings in period. Summer exhibition of paintings. *OPEN 10.00-17.00 Sat-Thur. Free.*

Osterley Park House

Thornbury Rd, Osterley, Middx. 01-560 3918. Remodelled by Robert Adam 1761-78 on an already fine Elizabethan building built round a courtyard. The magnificent interiors with furniture, mirrors, carpets and tapestry all show the elegance and richness of Adam's genius. *OPEN Apr-Sept 14.00-18.00; Oct-Mar 12.00-16.00. Admission in morning by special arrangement. CLOSED Mon (except B. hols). Charge. Park OPEN all year 10.00-dusk. Free.*

Oxford

A university city of spires and fine college buildings on the Thames and the Cherwell and dating from the 13th C. The Sheldonian Theatre by Wren, the Radcliffe Camera by Gibbs and the 15th C Bodleian Library are particularly notable. Visit also the famous old Botanic Garden and the Ashmolean Museum. Train 1½ hrs. *EC Thur.* London 65 miles (A40).

Sissinghurst Castle

Sissinghurst, Kent. Cranhurst 712850. The soft red-brick remains of the walls and buildings of a once extensive Tudor manor, enchantingly transformed by the late Victoria Sackville-West and Sir Harold Nicolson into numerous enclosed walled gardens. Each is different in character and outstandingly beautiful in its richness of flowers and shrubs. London 40 miles (A21). *OPEN 1st April-15th Oct 13.00-18.30 Mon-Fri, 10.00-18.30 weekends & B. hols. Charge. No dogs.*

Stratford-on-Avon, Warwicks

The birthplace of William Shakespeare (1564-1616). The town is still Elizabethan in atmosphere with overhung gables and timbered inns. Visit the poet's birthplace in Henley St, his house at New Place, Anne Hathaway's cottage and the museum and picture gallery. The Shakespeare Memorial Theatre in Waterside is thriving and progressive. Train 2½ hrs. *EC Thur.* London 90 miles (A40, A34).

Winchester, Hants

The ancient Saxon capital of England set among lovely rolling chalk downland. The massive, square towered Norman cathedral, with its superb vaulted Gothic nave, contains the graves of King Canute, Izaac Walton and Jane Austen. The 'round table of King Arthur' is in the remains of the Norman castle. Train 1½ hrs. *EC Thur.* London 65 miles (A30).

Windsor Castle

Windsor, Berks. Windsor 68286. An imposing 800-year-old medieval fortress. 12th C Round Tower built by Henry II. St George's chapel is fine 16th C perpendicular. Magnificent state apartments. *Castle precinct OPEN 10.00-sunset Mon-Sun all year. CLOSED Garter Day (2nd or 3rd Mon in Jun) and any State Visit arrival day. State Apartments OPEN May-Oct 10.30-17.00 Mon-Sat, 13.30-17.00 Sun; Nov-Apr 10.30-16.00 Mon-Sat. CLOSED when Queen is in residence — usually 6 weeks at Easter, 3 weeks in Jun and 3 weeks at Xmas. Charge.*

Woburn Abbey

Woburn, Beds. Woburn 666. The Duke of Bedford's 18th C mansion, set in a fine 3,000-acre park landscaped by Humphry Repton (part of which has been converted into a Safari Park). The house retains the quadrangular plan of the medieval monastery from which it also derived its site and name. Remodelling has occurred at different periods; the west front and the magnificent state apartments were done in 1747-60 by Henry Flitcroft; the south side, the lovely Chinese dairy and the orangery in 1802 by Henry Holland. Incomparable collection of pictures by Rembrandt, Van Dyck, Reynolds, Gainsborough, Holbein and a famous group of fine Canalettos. English and French furniture, porcelain and silver. London 40 miles (M1). *Abbey and Park OPEN Good Fri-Oct 31st 11.00-17.45 Mon-Sat, 11.00-18.15 Sun; OPEN Jan 1st, Feb 1st-Easter & Nov 13.00-16.45 Mon-Sun. Safari Park OPEN 10.00-18.00 or until dusk in winter. Charge.*

Information centres

These are the main sources of information available to the tourist about events, places or travel.

British Rail Travel Centre   **5 J 20**
4-12 Lower Regent St SW1. Personal callers only. British Rail's shop window in the West End. Booking centre for rail travel in Britain and rail-and-sea journeys to the Continent and Ireland. Several languages spoken. Smaller offices at: 14 Kingsgate Pde, Victoria St SW1, 407 Oxford St W1, 170b Strand WC2, 87 King William St EC4, Heathrow Airport.

City of London Information Centre   **6 M 28**
St Paul's Churchyard EC4. 01-606 3030. Information and advice with specific reference to the 'Square Mile'. Free literature. Monthly *Diary of Events* which lists a big choice of free entertainment in the City. *OPEN Apr-Sept 10.00-16.00 Mon-Sat; Oct-Mar 10.00-14.30. CLOSED 13.00-14.00.*

Daily Telegraph Information Bureau
Telephone only. 01-353 4242. General information service available *09.30-17.30 Mon-Fri.*

London Transport Travel Enquiry Offices
London Transport offices for enquiries on travel (underground and buses) and general tourist information. Their booklet *How to get there* is essential. Also free maps of underground and buses and tourist maps in foreign languages.
St James's Park Underground Station   **5 M 18**
01-222 1234, *24-hr telephone service*
And at the following underground stations:
Euston, Heathrow Central, King's Cross, Oxford Circus, Piccadilly Circus and Victoria.

National Tourist Information Centre   **5 M 15**
Main forecourt Victoria Station SW1. Gives travel and tourist information on London and England. Most languages spoken. Also instant hotel reservations, theatre and tour bookings, sales of tourist tickets, guide books and maps. *OPEN 09.00-20.30, 08.30-22.00 Jul & Aug.*
Telephone information service: 01-730 3488.
Harrods, Knightsbridge SW1   **2 I 12**
Heathrow Central Underground Station
Selfridges, Oxford St W1   **2 E 18**
Tower of London, West Gate E1   **6 R 31**

London tours
By coach
Sightseeing tours around the tourist attractions of central London and day trips to one or more sights outside London. London Transport do sightseeing tours without commentary and also sell special tickets for buses and tubes for the visitor who wants to find his own way around.

Evan Evans   **5 K 21**
37 Cockspur St SW1. 01-930 2377.

Frames   **3 F 25**
11 Herbrand St WC1. 01-837 6311.

National Tourist Information Centre   **5 M 15**
Main forecourt, Victoria Station SW1. Sell tickets for a selection of sightseeing tours.

London Transport Tours
Round London Sightseeing Tour – Mon-Sun every hour from Grosvenor Gdns Victoria, Eros Piccadilly, and Marble Arch, *from 09.00-16.00.* Coaches, double-deckers and open-topped buses when the sun shines. Covers 20 miles of the City and West End.
Official Guided Coach Tours – guided half-day and day tours round London and day tours out of London, starting from LT Coach Station Wilton Rd SW1. Check times and book at any LT Travel Information Centre, or Victoria Coach Station.

London Transport Special Tickets
London Explorer Pass – Valid for travel on the tube in central and inner London and on all LT buses. Available for one, three, four or seven days. *Red Rover* – a day's unlimited travel on London's red buses. *Reduced price for children.* Zonal Travelcards also facilitate economic travel on both bus and underground. From travel enquiry offices, underground stations and bus garages.

The Park Lane Sightseeing Company   **2 I 14**
93 Knightsbridge SW1. 01-235 0267. Luxury tours of London. Also tours of Oxford, Stratford, Blenheim Palace and Windsor. First class service.

By private guides
To locate a London Tourist Board registered guide, contact your travel agent or the LTB.

Autoguide   **2 I 14**
19-23 Knightsbridge SW1. 01-235 0806. Any sort of tour arranged, from a two-hour shopping trip to a Continental jaunt. Most European languages spoken.

British Tours   **2 F 19**
6 South Molton St W1. 01-926 5267. Wide variety of individual tours throughout London and surrounding areas with qualified driver/guides and under-graduate couriers.

Prestige London Taxi Guides
18 Monterey Clo, Bexley, Kent. 01-584 3118. Personal sightseeing service by licensed London taxidrivers who are also Tourist Board registered guides. *24-hr booking service.*

By foot
Canal Walks
Inland Waterways Association 01-286 6101 or British Waterways Board 01-262 6711. Two alternative walks along the Regent's Canal, starting from Camden Town tube station, then either west to Little Venice or east to the City Road Basin.

Discovering London
11 Pennyfield, Warley, Brentwood, Essex. Brentwood 213704. Many walks, including: Jack the Ripper, Evil London, Night Prowl, Ghosts and Pubs, Great Fire. Leaflet giving details and times from the above or from LTB and City Information Centre.

Hidden London   **6 L 29**
102 Newgate St EC1. 01-600 8244. Three-hr tours of little known parts of London that even Londoners may not know. *10.30 Tue-Sat* from Holborn tube station.

The Londoners
3 Springfield Av N10. 01-883 2656. Pub tours, various routes; Bankside, Covent Garden, Rother-hithe. Visit four or five pubs. From Temple tube station *19.30 Fri.*

London Walks
139 Conway Rd, Southgate N14. 01-882 2763. Meet at various tube stations for topical walks through London lasting $1\frac{1}{2}$-2hrs. 40 different walks offered. Titles include Dickens' London, Ghosts of the West End. *Phone for details. Children (accompanied) free.*

Theatreland Tours   **5 J 22**
11 Goodwin's Ct WC2. 01-240 0915. Tours of the Covent Garden area, including backstage visit to a West End theatre, for groups of 12 or more. *Mornings Mon-Sat, afternoons Mon-Fri.*

INFORMATION

Hotel booking agents

Accommodation Service of the National Tourist Information Centre   **5 M 15**
Tourist Information Centre, main forecourt, Victoria Station SW1. No phone. They give information and make bookings. *OPEN 09.00-20.30 Mon-Sat. Longer hours in summer*. Also at Heathrow.

Balcombe Bureau   **2 A 18**
86 Balcombe St NW1. 01-262 6688. Hotel reservations in London and Britain. All classes of hotels. Also holiday flats arranged. *OPEN 08.00-18.00 Mon-Sat*.

Concordia   **5 N 16**
19 Churton St SW1. 01-834 7673. All kinds of hotels. *OPEN 09.00-17.00 Mon-Fri. Free*.

Eco-Res   **2 B 13**
3 Spring St W2. 01-262 2601. Hotel bookings in London and throughout Britain. Specialise in exhibitions. *OPEN 09.30-18.00 Mon-Fri*.

Expotel Hotel Reservations
Dial 01-568 8765 to make hotel reservations. Covers the whole of Great Britain. *OPEN 09.00-17.30 Mon-Fri. Free*.

Hotel Booking Service   **2 H 20**
Cashmere House, 13-14 Golden Sq W1. 01-437 5052. Excellent and knowledgeable service to business firms and general public. All types of hotel reservations in London, UK and worldwide. *OPEN 09.30-17.30 Mon-Fri. Charge for private bookings*.

Hotel Finders
20 Bell La NW4. 01-202 0988. All kinds of hotels. *OPEN 09.00-17.30 Mon-Fri, to 16.00 Sat*.

Hotel Guide   **2 I 22**
Faraday House, 8-10 Charing Cross Rd WC2. 01-836 7677. First class hotel accommodation service. *OPEN 09.00-17.30 Mon-Fri. Free*.

Hotel Pacc Group Services Ltd   **5 L 15**
10 Lower Belgrave St SW1. 01-730 7148. Hotel accommodation for groups (10 people or more) in London and Europe. Facilities for coach and tour operators and conference organisers. *OPEN 09.30-17.30 Mon-Fri*.

Note
It is compulsory for hotels to display their prices.

Visitors should make sure exactly what is included in the price, ie. breakfast, VAT, service, etc. Many hotels have facilities for conferences, banquets, receptions, etc.

Tipping

Should be an expression of pleasure for service rendered and never a duty and it is still possible to not tip at all if the circumstances justify this. These guidelines give some idea of the average tip:

Restaurants Many now add on a service charge, usually 10%, but do not always say so — if in doubt ask them. They usually say if it is not included. 10% is the minimum, give up to 15% for above average service.

Taxis 10-15%.

Women's hairdressers 15% to the hairdresser, 5% to the shampooer.

Men's hairdressers 15%.

Cloakroom attendants 10p per article when collected.

Washroom services 10p if individual attention is given.

Commissionaires For getting a taxi. From nothing to 40p depending on the effort expended.

Pubs and bars Never at the bar but buy the barman a drink if you wish. For waiter service in the lounge, from 10p per drink.

Hotels Almost all add it to your bill, usually 15%. Give· extra to individuals for special service, from 50p.

Porters from 20p-30p per case depending on how far it is carried.

Telephone services

All London telephone numbers begin with 01-followed by seven figures. If already in London do not dial the 01, only the seven following figures. If dialling from London to the exchange elsewhere, you must find the code of the exchange. The codes are listed in a booklet called Telephone Dialling Codes or the operator will tell you. If dialling from a coin box telephone, dial as normal and when a connection is made rapid pips will sound; insert money — either 5p or 10p. Pips will repeat at intervals and more money must then be inserted to continue the connection. Details of all telephone services are in the booklet — this is a summary.

Emergency calls Dial 999 and ask for police, fire or ambulance service.
Directory enquiries 142 for London postal addresses, 192 for other British addresses.
Transfer charge (collect) calls or difficulty in getting through to a number — 100 for the operator.
Telegrams 190 for inland, 193 for international.
International calls You can now dial direct to many countries. Codes are listed in the *Telephone Dialling Codes* booklet or ask the operator.
Recorded services:
Puffin Storyline 246 8000. **Bedtime stories** *from 18.00.*
Childrens' London 246 8007.
Discline *18.00-08.00 Mon-Fri and all Sat, Sun.* 160.
Financial Times Index and Business News Summary 246 8026.
Radioline 246 8035.
Traveline 246 8021. Motoring information.
Racing results 168
Recipe for the day 246 8071.
Leisureline Tourist information. 246 8041.
Time 123.
Weather forecast 246 8091.

Passports

Passport office   **5 L 18**
Clive House, Petty France SW1. 01-213 3000. *OPEN 09.00-16.30 Mon-Fri. Emergencies 16.30-18.00 Mon-Fri, 10.00-12.00 Sat.*
Immigration Office
Lunar House, Wellesley Rd, Croydon, Surrey. 01-686 0688. Deals with questions concerning the granting of British visas to foreigners and entry under the Commonwealth Immigration Act. Subject to approval, visas are then supplied by the
Foreign Office   **5 L 18**
Clive House, Petty France SW1. 01-233 3000.

Tourist offices

Britain   **5 J 19**
British Tourist Authority, 64 St James's St SW1. 01-499 9325.
Ireland   **2 H 19**
Irish Tourist Office, Ireland House, 150 New Bond St W1. 01-493 3201.
Jersey   **5 K 21**
Jersey Tourist Information Office, 118 Grand Buildings, Trafalgar Sq WC2. 01-930 1619.

Northern Ireland   **2 I 18**
Northern Ireland Tourist Board, 11 Berkeley St W1.
01-493 0601.

Scotland   **5 K 21**
Scottish Tourist Board, 19 Cockspur St SW1. 01-930
8661.

Wales   **2 G 19**
Wales Tourist Board, 2-4 Maddox St W1. 01-409
0969.

Foreign exchange facilities

*The principal clearing banks and their branches
throughout London are always very willing to help
overseas visitors. Some banks have special travel
departments. Travellers cheques may be exchanged
at any time during normal banking hours:
09.30-15.30 Mon-Fri.*

*Many of the principal London hotels operate their
own foreign exchange facilities for the convenience
of their guests. The rates of commission are
generally a little higher than those of banks.*

*Many bureau de change open until late but often
charge high commission. The following places open
later than usual as do the banks at Heathrow and
Gatwick airports.*

American Express   **5 J 21**
6 Haymarket SW1. 01-930 4411. *OPEN 09.00-17.00
Mon-Fri, 09.00-18.00 Sat, 10.00-18.00 Sun.* 78
Brompton Rd SW3. 01-584 6182. *OPEN
09.00-17.00 Mon-Fri, 09.00-12.00 Sat.*

Barclays Bank
Brent Cross Shopping Centre NW4. 01-202 3311.
OPEN 09.30-20.00 Mon-Fri, 09.00-18.00 Sat.

Chequepoint   **5 J 21**
37 Coventry St W1. 01-839 3772. Also 236 Earl's
Court Rd SW5. 01-370 3239. Will cash cheques
backed by a cheque card. Higher percentage charge
made between *24.00 & 08.00. OPEN 24 hrs Mon-
Sun.* Twelve other branches throughout West End,
OPEN 08.30-24.00.

Erskine Bureaux   **1 B 11**
22 Leinster Ter W2. 01-402 6305. Various other
branches in London. *OPEN 08.00-20.00 daily.*

Thomas Cook   **5 M 17**
100 Victoria St SW1. 01-828 0437. *OPEN
09.00-17.00 Mon-Fri, 09.00-12.00 Sat.*
104 Kensington High St W8. 01-937 3673. *OPEN
09.00-17.00 Mon-Sat.*
Victoria Station   **5 M 15**
SW1. *OPEN daily 07.45-22.00.*

Emergencies

Accident
*Most large general hospitals have a casualty depart-
ment but they are not always open 24 hrs. In an
emergency or accident, wherever you are, dial 999.
The operator will give you the name of the nearest
hospital casualty department open at that time and
probably arrange an ambulance if necessary.*

All-night prescription
*Your local police station keep a list of chemists and
doctors available at all hours. Or try:*

Bliss Chemist
54 Willesden La NW6. 01-624 8000. *24 hrs.*

V. J. Hall   2 I 21
85 Shaftesbury Av W1. 01-437 3174. *OPEN
09.30-23.00 Mon-Sat, 12.00-22.00 Sun.*

Broken down?
AA Breakdown service
01-954 7373. *24 hrs.*

RAC Breakdown service
(92) 33555 (north of the Thames). 01-681 3611
(south of the Thames). *24 hrs.*

Late post?
Post office   5 J 22
St Martin's Pl, Trafalgar Sq WC2. 01-930 9580.
*OPEN 08.00-20.00 Mon-Sat, 10.00-17.00 Sun &
B. hols. CLOSED Xmas.*

Transport
*The underground system closes down about mid-
night and there's often a long wait for late night
buses. There are fewer taxis around late at night and
prices increase after midnight. Minicabs operate
24-hr services and the* Yellow Pages *is full of them.
But for the more affluent try:*

Avis Rent-a-Car   2 E 17
68 North Row, Marble Arch W1. 01-629 7811. *24-hr
service from Heathrow and Gatwick airports.*

Godfrey Davis Europe Car   5 M 16
Davis House, Wilton Rd SW1. 01-834 8484. *OPEN
08.00-20.00 Mon-Sun.*
London Heathrow Airport. 01-897 0811. Desks in
each terminal. *24 hr service Mon-Sun.*